AF325816

Was Muhammad crazy?

Frédéric Joi

WAS MUHAMMAD CRAZY?

Max Milo

Max Milo Editions
Collection Essais-Documents, Paris, 2023
www.maxmilo.com
EAN : 9782315011100

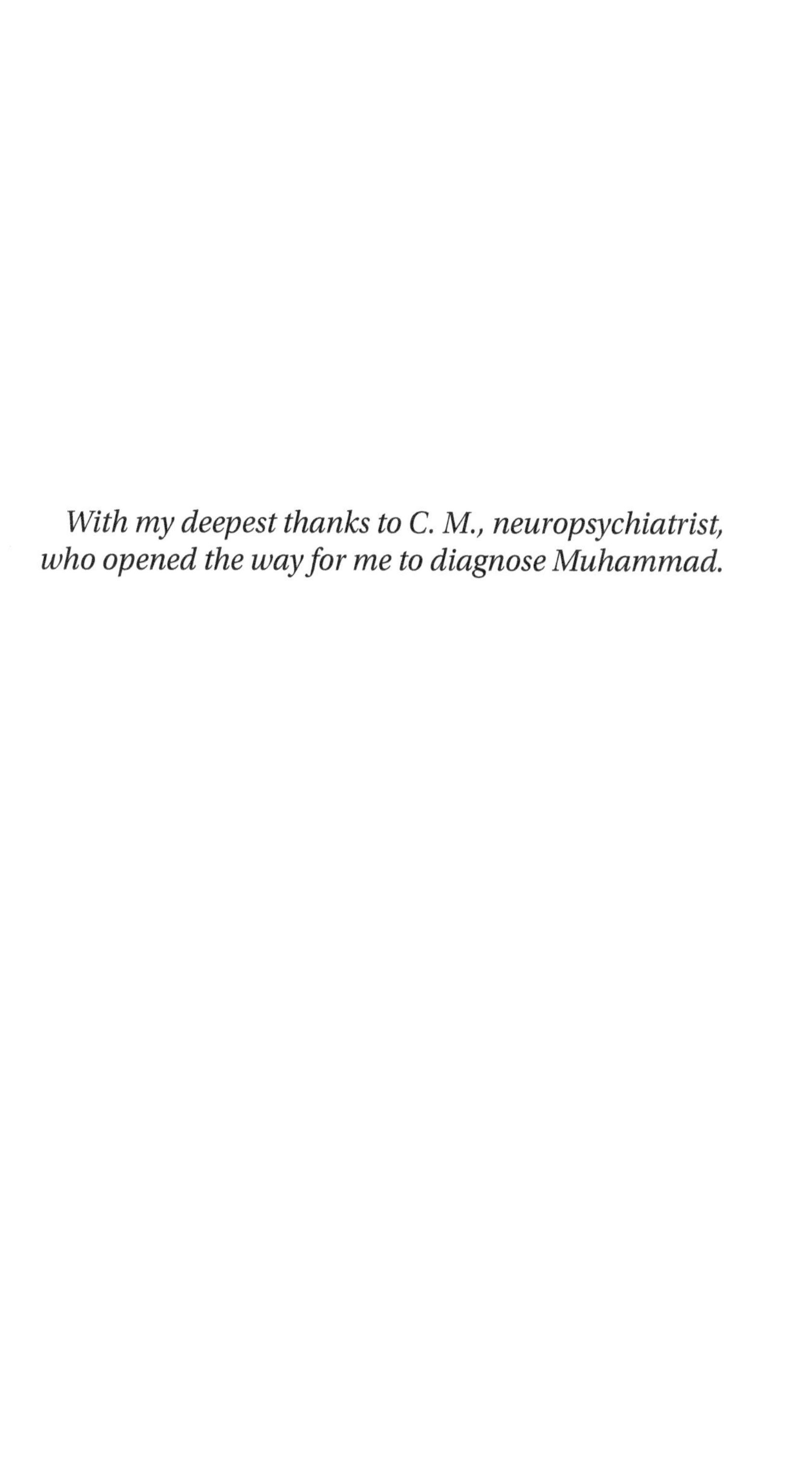

With my deepest thanks to C. M., neuropsychiatrist, who opened the way for me to diagnose Muhammad.

PUBLISHER'S DISCLAIMER

Dear reader, dear friend of all faiths, relax and smile: this book does not take itself seriously. Its project, launched two years ago, is an act of collective resistance, especially through humor, against any overflow of religious discourse in the social field. It is not the effect of a partisan ideology, but works modestly for critical freedom and joy in the world. It is not born from a desire to offend, but from a firm concern to defend a plural universe where no one is physically threatened for his or her ideas, be they false, daring or burlesque. These lines are part of the outraged tradition of the pamphlet inherited from the rationalism of the Enlightenment. The work follows an equally iconoclastic *Jesus*, and we should not forget that the enlightened West did not fail in the eighteenth and nineteenth centuries to attack the excesses of its own Judeo-Christianity and its hegemonic temptations. We believe with the author that the risk for the Churches themselves is to border on fundamentalism, as illustrated by the excesses of Christianity, Hinduism or any other form of confusion between faith and the government of a people. It is not a question of playing the West against the East, but rather tolerance against fear, the pen against the sword and humor against seriousness. Was it necessary to give up publishing this long-planned text in view of recent events? No, because when it comes to religious extremism, nothing is really new under the sun, and for thousands of years, people have been killed or scorned for nothing. It is precisely the purpose of this book to show the face that faith takes on when it loses its reason: deformed. What are distorting mirrors for? Children know: to laugh at themselves.

INTRODUCTION

"We will always ignore his deep psychology in detail."

Maxime Rodinson[1]

Muhammad is a fascinating being.

He first fascinated some of his contemporaries in his home town, Mecca.

Then he fascinated whole crowds in his host city, Medina, and in the Arabian Peninsula during his lifetime.

In the space of a few decades, he went from being a starving orphan to a powerful warlord, rich and surrounded by beautiful women. He unified the Arab world, previously torn apart by constant clan rivalries.

And above all, the crowds considered him nothing less than the messenger of God.

After his death, his reputation grew even more. Over the centuries, he fascinated billions of people,

1. RODINSON (Maxime), *Muhammad*, Paris, Éditions du Seuil, 1994, p. 77.

who chose him as their spiritual guide and followed his model of political leadership.

Muhammad is a fascinating being.

A Western atheist of the 21st century cannot fail to be surprised. As with Jesus and the Christians[2], we would like to understand such a historical phenomenon. Today we have new analytical tools that should allow us to shed unexpected light on a character so far removed from us. The human sciences have made extraordinary progress. History, sociology, psychology, political science, psychiatry, psychoanalysis, philosophy, anthropology, etc., offer us as many analytical grids that allow us to hope to pierce the veil of the centuries and of human passions.

A host of questions then arise. How can we understand these mystical crises, during which Muhammad heard Gabriel speaking to him in the name of God? How can we interpret his incredible vindictiveness, which allowed him to raise the Arab world? Where does his sense of order come from, which he was able to impose on a stateless people? What is the origin of his querulous character, which made him revolt against injustices and institute new rules? How can we explain his special relationship with previous prophets? Where did his religious knowledge come from? How did he manage to make himself obeyed by a quarrelsome people?

More generally, how can we understand that he was able to lead his contemporaries, *a priori* reluctant, followed by countless followers over the centuries, to

------

2. See JOI (Frédéric), *Jésus était-il fou ?*, Paris, Max Milo, 2010.

die for his ideas? How could his words have influenced the course of history and still fascinate hundreds of millions of people today?

From a scientific point of view, we must go beyond the answers based on the existence of God. The contemporary atheist must enlighten by the Lights of reason this mystical phenomenon whose ultimate repercussions still weigh on our modern world.

By way of background, for the benefit of Westerners, we would like to offer a summary of the life of Muhammad and the book that came out of his "revelations".

We can divide his life of about sixty years into four periods: his youth (twenty-five years), his first marriage (about fifteen years), his revelations in Mecca (about twelve years) and his exile in Medina, with the recapture of Mecca (about ten years).

Around 570-571, Muhammad was born in what is now Saudi Arabia, on the side of Mecca. At that time, the Arab population was composed of traders, sedentary peasants and nomadic Bedouins[3]. Without a central state, they lived according to a clan system, regulated by a code of honor, consisting of vendettas, raids, incessant wars, and the enslavement of the defeated. The historian, sociologist and orientalist Maxime Rodinson evokes a "low level in the scale of civilizations" due to "the social situation of the time, within the framework of the extremely bad natural conditions of the Arabian Peninsula. Hunger is never

---

3. See in particular RODINSON (Maxime), *op. cit.* chapter II, "Presentation of a land".

a good advisor and the Arabs were often hungry"[4]. The infant mortality rate was very high. Marriages were arranged between families according to clan interests, with very young girls having limited rights. The Arabs of this period mixed polytheism and superstition. The Bible was not well known, only through the Christians and Jews, who were in the minority.

Muhammad belonged to a clan responsible for a high religious site, the "Ka'ba", in Mecca. Their clan name can be translated into French in different ways: "Quraych"[5], "Quraysh"[6], "Quraïch"[7] or "Qoraysh"[8]. Muhammad was orphaned, raised by a wet nurse and then by other family members. At the age of eight, his uncle Abû Tâlib took him under his wing and took him on a trade caravan to Syria.

Around 595, at the age of twenty-five, Muhammad entered into a profitable marriage with a wealthy woman in her forties, Khadijah bint Khowaylid. They had many children, but no boys survived. Muhammad meditated in ascetic retreats in a cave and learned about religions from random travelers. This was reflected in the quality of his religious knowledge. He also traded as a couple with his wife, and proved to

---

4. *Ibid*, p. 39.
5. By Wahib Atallah in his translation of HICHAM (Ibn), *La Biographie du prophète*, Paris, Fayard, 2004.
6. By HUSSEIN (Mahmoud), *Al-Sîra. Le prophète de l'Islam raconté par ses compagnons*, Paris, Grasset et Fasquelle, 2005, collection " Hachette Littérature ", volumes I and II.
7. By Denise Masson in her translation of the *Koran*, Paris, Gallimard-NRF, coll. "La Pléiade", 1967-2007.
8. By RODINSON (Maxime), *op. cit.*

be a competent businessman, thanks in part to his organized character and integrity.

In 610, around the age of 40, Muhammad was struck by "revelations" (*Ayat*, "signs from God") in which he saw the angel Gabriel. At first he did not understand, and had strong doubts. His wife encouraged him. Gabriel often came back to visit him, and declared him to be a messenger of the one God of the Bible, whose content he repeated as faithfully as possible. Three years later, he began to talk to people about his mission and tried to convince his relatives. In ten years he converted only about a hundred Meccans. In the early days, he enjoyed the protection of his uncle, a clan leader. When his uncle died, Muhammad became increasingly oppressed. He even sent a small delegation of his new converts to Abyssinia, and occasionally had to take refuge in a nearby cave or oasis.

In 622, in his fifties, Muhammad went into exile further north, to Medina (then known as Yathrib) with a few dozen followers. This was the hegira (flight) which marked the beginning of the Islamic era. Muhammad depended on the local Jews, who were initially rather favorable to part of his monotheistic message. But later on, these Jews criticized Muhammad's vague knowledge. Muhammad became annoyed at their mockery. He proposed other laws and behaviors (of rituals, dress, etc.). When he gained power and confidence, he criticized them in return, accusing them of not being faithful to their own book, which he claimed to defend better. At the end of this reversal[9] of

---

9. See RODINSON (Maxime), *op. cit.* p. 220.

relations, he had these many Jews killed, as they had become opponents in this host city. How did he reach a dominant position, when his small community was so poor? He began by organizing small raids for loot. Then he attacked the caravans coming from Mecca. He started a war with the Meccans, including members of his own clan. He converted people by force or persuasion. His increasing success enabled him to enter into several marriages. He had many children, but still no viable sons. He also focused on gaining power within the city through targeted assassinations and tribal conversions. With his new and growing following, he was able to reconquer Mecca by the sheer deterrence of an army of at least ten thousand men. He unified the Arabs under Islam, overcoming clan systems of revenge and honor.

After his death in Medina in 632, when he was in his sixties, the Muslim community ('Umma) covered almost the entire Arabian Peninsula. Great conquests followed. But clan traditions had not disappeared, and were instead encouraged, codified, and legitimized by a supreme justification, that of the existence of an absolute father. In the past, clans had fought among themselves, with political decisions spread out among chiefs. After Muhammad, they attacked other peoples in an organized and unified way with new religious convictions. They mixed politics, religion, law, family privacy, and submitted to single rulers modeled on Muhammad - caliphs originally, heads of state more recently.

Let us now summarize this tool of Arab unification, the Qur'an - its extremely repetitive nature makes this task easier. It was written under Muhammad's dictation, following his revelations, on different media that were compiled years later. Curiously, these revelations, in the form of suras (chapters), were arranged in descending order of length, not in historical order. But their chronological evolution can be summarized by two periods, which correspond to his revelations in Mecca and those in Medina. In the first period, "... the preaching of the supreme truths about divinity, the world and man, the call to the inner reformation of each one, the teaching of the history of the divine action towards mankind..."[10], in other words: "In the beginning, the Voice expounded to the Arabs a universal message already known by others."[11] In the second period, "it was necessary above all to mobilize energies for immediate action, to denounce the enemy, to comfort the faithful troops, to justify the decisions taken, to stigmatize the traitors and the hesitators, to give rules of life to the community of believers. [...] one finds lengthy and stringy articles of code, exhortations, protests, proclamations of an often painful prosaic nature, cluttered with repetitions and stylistic errors"[12], in other words: "It is addressed to a particular community [...]" [13]

---

10. RODINSON (Maxime), *op. cit.* p. 251.
11. *Ibid,* p. 271.
12. *Ibid,* p. 251
13. *Ibid,* p. 271.

Most of the time, his style was of a high poetry. "Perhaps no language is more conducive to spontaneous poetry than Arabic"[14], which gives it a haunting character[15]. This point ruins from the outset any idea of universality, as the literary form of this text does not translate well. The Arabs would gain much by reading the Koran in another language, in order to concentrate on its content. We will voluntarily refer to the pagination of a French translation[16], and not to the numbering of suras and verses.

Let's turn to its content.

The Qur'an contains three kinds of considerations.

First, he speaks of God and the prophets of the Bible, in edifying accounts. Muhammad repeated over and over that he was the one sent by God. The other prophets of the Bible would have preceded him, and he would remain the last. Jesus would only be one of them, not the son of God. The latter would be unique, omniscient, omnipotent and the cause of everything. A paradise and a hell would be promised respectively to those who obey and those who disobey.

Then he sets out laws to be followed. They are taken from the Bible and from Arab tradition, then distorted and arranged by him. These laws are accompanied by exhortations to obey them, not to say aggressive threats. Muhammad laid down a host of precepts, such as the number of daily prayers, the kind of food that was permissible, the number of wives allowed, how

---

14. *Ibid*, p. 122.
15. *Ibid*, p. 123.
16. *The Koran, op. cit.*

they should be treated, some basic economic rules (such as the prohibition of interest-bearing loans), and so on. He claimed to be right about everything, and continually boasted of being right.

Finally, the Qur'an contains the little stories of the community, including encouragement to fight.

CHAPTER ONE
THE MYSTICAL CRISES OF MUHAMMAD

"You think he is crazy. No, he is not a madman; we know what madness is, with its signs of confusion and rambling."
Al-Nadr ibn al-Hârith[17]

Let us begin our investigation by the very heart of Islam. Muhammad claimed to hear the voice of God or Gabriel, during very particular crises. We have many descriptive passages of these revelations, which appeared to him in his forties (in 612, in Mecca). They did not leave him until his death, some twenty years later, although the intensity and duration seem to have diminished during his life. Let us note a badly dated event, during his childhood in the desert, when two angels came to "open his chest", to remove his heart, to clean it, to weigh it, and to put it back in its place!

---

17. Quoted in HUSSEIN (Mahmoud), *op. cit.* volume I, p. 366.

We have little information about his childhood[18]. We know that his father 'Abdallah died around the time of his birth, and that his mother Âmina died when he was only six years old[19]. In accordance with tradition, he was entrusted in his early childhood by his mother and the Quraysh to a wet nurse, Halima, from a nomadic clan, the Banu Sa'd[20]. The very young Muhammad was educated in the desert[21]. When his mother died, his eighty-year-old grandfather 'Abd al-Mottalib took him in and died himself two years later. Muhammad was orphaned for the third time, so to speak. His uncle, 'Abd Manaf, also called 'Abû Tâlib, took care of the child. "But 'Abû Tâlib was in need and his children did not always eat enough. Sometimes Muhammad slept on an empty stomach and wept silently.[22] The cultural and geographical context confirms that food was still a scarce commodity. We can reasonably imagine that an orphan might have been educated "the hard way," beaten, or malnourished, especially in years of increased drought.

Let's go straight to his forties. Here are some descriptions of these crises:

"Mohammad's face was covered with sweat, he was shaking with chills, he remained unconscious for an

18. See in particular HICHÂM (Ibn), *op. cit.* p. 25; RODINSON (Maxime), *op. cit.* p. 66.
19. *Ibid.*
20. See in particular Rodinson (Maxime), *op. cit.* pp. 67 ff. It should be noted that this same clan is described as a "sedentary country" in HICHAM (Ibn), *op. cit.* p. 54.
21. See in particular RODINSON (Maxime), *op. cit.* pp. 67-69.
22. HUSSEIN (Mahmoud), *op. cit.* volume I, p. 222.

hour, as if in a state of intoxication. He could not hear what was being said to him. He was sweating profusely, even in cold weather. He heard strange noises, like chains or bells or the rustle of wings. "Not once," he said, "was a revelation made to me without my thinking that my soul was being taken away." [23]

"At the moment when the phenomenon [of revelation] is going to manifest itself, he hears a buzzing sound: sometimes similar to that of a swarm of bees rushing out of the hive and sometimes more metallic like the ringing of a bell. [His companions could notice each time [...] the sudden paleness followed by a congested redness of Muhammad's face. Moreover, he himself was aware of this, since he ordered that his head be covered with a veil each time the phenomenon occurred. [...] Doesn't this precaution mean that this phenomenon was independent of the man's will, since he was momentarily paralyzed, unable to cover his own face and groaning in an extremely painful state... Only the face is congested: the man's attitude is normal and, in any case, his intellectual freedom is well marked, from the psychological point of view, by the fact that Muhammad makes perfect use of his memory during the crisis itself. Several historical events in the phenomenon of prophecy seem to be completely out of his own control [...] " [24]

"The Messenger of God did not move. But suddenly he was seized with the usual symptoms of revelation.

---

23. RODINSON (Maxime), *op. cit.* p. 100.
24. BENNABI (Malek), *Le Phénomène coranique*, Paris, legal deposit no 67 B 1709, ᵃquarter, 1976, p. 77.

He was laid down, his cloak was thrown over him, and a leather pillow was put under his head. [The Prophet finally woke up and sat up. His forehead was beaded as on a rainy day."[25] Afterwards, apparently, he was able to leave his house and go out to meet people, in other words, he did not show any confusion after the seizure.

Faced with this phenomenon, which was disconcerting to say the least, Muhammad, like his contemporaries, was initially perplexed. They could not but be unaware of its true nature, but tried to interpret it from the categories at their disposal.

Regarding his childhood seizure, "his Christian enemies saw it as epilepsy"[26].

At the beginning of Muhammad's revelations, his Quraysh tribesmen deliberated about what to tell the Arab world before the season of pilgrimage. They considered whether he was a diviner, a madman, a poet or a sorcerer[27]. The poet was considered to be inspired by the jinn (demons)[28]. Let us also note that "the Quraysh used to insult the Prophet and call him "Mudhammam" ("the madman")"[29]. As with Jesus, there is a particular lucidity among those who knew him well, both before and after the arrival of the revelations. Let us note this mediation proposal tried with Muhammad by a rich notable of his Quraysh clan,

25. HICHÂM (Ibn), *op. cit.* pp. 297-298.
26. RODINSON (Maxime), *op. cit.* p. 81.
27. See HICHÂM (Ibn), *op. cit.* p. 92. See the rejection of these options in HUSSEIN (Mahmud), *op. cit.* volume I, p. 366.
28. *Ibid*, note p. 310.
29. HICHÂM (Ibn), *op. cit.* p. 124.

during the period of Mecca: "[...] if this being that haunts you and obsesses you is a jinn from which you cannot get rid of it, we will consult doctors and spend our fortune to cure you of it."[30] His contemporaries still considered him a pretender, or in their words, a "liar"[31]. Still at that time, several tribes had their own "prophet", so this category was also available[32].

He himself struggled to understand his own crises, especially in the early days. "Muhammad began to hear voices, which addressed him as "Muhammad". He searched for the origin of these voices, but could not find anything. He became frightened and tried to run away. [He would say to his wife Khadijah, "I am afraid I will lose my mind.[33] He did not want to identify himself with a poet or a man possessed, and several times considered committing suicide by throwing himself off a hill[34]. His wife supported him, convinced of his "goodness. Several times in the Qur'an he justified himself as not being mad or possessed, sometimes through the account of a prophet like Noah[35].

In order to understand himself, he still considered the category of "kâhin", only to push it back[36]. The kâhin were "diviners of the desert, also on their way to the slopes of mystical ascent", who expressed

---

30. *Ibid*, p. 98.
31. HUSSEIN (Mahmoud), *op. cit.* volume I, p. 467.
32. *Ibid*, p. 290.
33. *Ibid*, pp. 304-305.
34. HUSSEIN (Mahmoud), *op. cit.* volume I, pp. 310 and 314.
35. See in particular *The Qur'an, op. cit*, Sura VII, verse 66, p. 189, and verse 184, p. 209.
36. See RODINSON (Maxime), *op. cit.* p. 108.

themselves "in short, breathless sentences, no doubt ejected in violent jerks, with more or less rich rhymes [...] which in Arabic is called 'saj' or rhymed prose"[37].

Finally, the Arabs of the time had a wide choice of categories to account for such an unusual phenomenon. Was Muhammad an epileptic, a seer (kahin), a madman, a poet inspired by a jinn, a sorcerer, a prophet, possessed or insane?

Even though this last category would tend to impose itself naturally today, the contemporary tools of psychiatry require and allow a much more precise diagnosis. In a first, spontaneous approach, what could we say about such states?

Epilepsy seems to be ruled out from the start, because of the absence of confusion after the seizure. It consists of an electrochemical dysfunction of the brain, in paroxysmal hyperactivity, which does not allow to listen to precise voices nor to remember them.

Like Malek Bennabi, we discard schizophrenia[38]. This corresponds to a permanent state, installed, where the individual is clearly cut off from social reality. Schizophrenics are also characterized by the invention of a universe of their own, contrary to Muhammad who constantly referred to the Bible. We still agree with this author when he speaks of prophetism as an objective phenomenon independent of the human "self" that expresses itself. Indeed, Muhammad did not seem to control these crises nor this voice, especially in his first period in Mecca. He

---

37. *Ibid*, p. 108.
38. See BENNABI (Malek), *op. cit.*

seems to us to be quite sincere, in good faith, himself having resisted it as much as possible, for years, before giving in to it.

Such symptoms could still make one think of chronic migraines. But from a psychological point of view, this last hypothesis would not allow us to go any further in interpreting this inner voice, so particular, precise and rich in organized meanings.

Finally, the use of substances could trigger such seizures, which would be of an "intoxicating" nature. We cannot totally eliminate this hypothesis. But there is not the slightest allusion, even indirect, to the taking of any substance, either in the Koran or in the numerous accounts of the companions of the person concerned[39].

The mystery thickens. What were these crises and this inner voice, independent of his will?

The American Psychiatric Association publishes and regularly updates an authoritative *Diagnostic and Statistical Manual of Mental Disorders.* This manual distinguishes fifteen categories of mental illness, among which are "dissociative disorders", which correspond to one of the possible aspects of the old name "hysteria". It differentiates five types of dissociative disorders: dissociative amnesia, dissociative fugue, depersonalization disorder, dissociative disorder not otherwise specified, and "dissociative identity disorder", abbreviated to DID, formerly

---

39. See in particular HICHAM (Ibn), *op. cit.* and HUSSEIN (Mahmoud), *op. cit.*

known as "multiple personality". This disorder affects less than 1% of the population.

The way Americans currently interpret the latter disease is based on the work of the French psychologist Pierre Janet, from the end of the 19th century. He conceived normal consciousness as a synthesis of psychological functions: perceptions, memories, movements, ideas, emotions or organic sensations (hunger, excretion, etc.). Current researchers relate this conception to "modular" neurobiology. Each "module" represents a distinct part of the brain that deals specifically with one of these functions.

In dissociative disorders, certain functions become separated from the "self". The subject can no longer say that he sees or hears, he becomes "blind", "deaf", he loses control of a limb, etc. These functions are no longer integrated into the self.

In the absence of correct treatment, this dissociation worsens. Other functions separate from the self, from the main identity of the subject, to regroup in a second identity. This one becomes more and more autonomous. It is formed little by little in a coherent way, but separated, as the personality of a child is constituted. This is the IDD. By a sordid effect of communicating vessels, the second identity is reinforced by emptying the first of its functions. The two identities become independent, and can no longer appear at the same time, under the same consciousness. They take it in turns to control the subject's behavior.

Symptoms commonly noted by psychiatrists include: dissimilar attitudes and beliefs, unexplained migraines, various other somatic pains, distortion or loss of sense of time, sudden angers with no apparent cause, ability to speak of oneself by a plural ("we" or "they"), The patient may also experience "derealization" (perception of familiar people or the environment as if they were unknown or imaginary), "depersonalization" (a feeling of unreality, of detachment from oneself and one's own physical and mental processes, the patient feels like an observer of oneself, he/she has the impression that he/she no longer occupies his/her body), etc. Insofar as the various identities often interact with each other, the patient reports having heard inner conversations between other people, which are directly addressed to him or her. Although these voices are experienced as hallucinations, they are very different from those of psychotic disorders such as schizophrenia. Before the 19th century in the West, these symptoms were interpreted as possession by a spirit. Many patients abuse illicit or psychoactive substances at the same time.

Janet had already partly identified the causes of such a condition. Dissociative identity disorders are most often caused by a "chronic" (i.e., non-specific) trauma in early childhood, such as a recurrent rape, a natural disaster with lasting effects, a serious accident, a bereavement (death of a parent), under-nutrition, or repeated violence (child beating, for a large percentage of DID). The young child takes refuge in his or her own thoughts, in which he or she forgets the traumatic situation.

This disorder does not heal spontaneously. The medical reference book for the diagnosis and therapeutic treatment of all illnesses, the Merck Manual, recommends that the identities be made to interact and work together. Hypnosis, as practiced by Janet, can contribute to this, by going back more quickly to the causes of dissociation. Then, the psychiatrist tries to reconnect the identities and integrate them into social relationships.

Freud had also begun to use hypnosis to find the traumatic causes of hysterics, notably with the famous Anna O. case.[40] Judging that one did not go far enough into the patient's unconscious, he had invented the technique of associations of ideas, known as free associations, in other words psychoanalysis. For him, hysterics suffer from reminiscences (repressed memories), linked to a trauma, most often sexual, during childhood[41]. They use their body as a means of expression of this unconscious conflict. In their symptomatology, they seem to imitate other illnesses, such as epilepsy, paralysis of the limbs, or nowadays rather spasmophilia, skin pathologies, etc. Freud points out

---

40. See BREUER and FREUD (Sigmund), *Études sur l'hystérie* (1895), Paris, PUF, coll. " Bibliothèque de psychanalyse ", 1992, in particular pp. 14-35. For a summary, see FREUD (Sigmund), *Cinq leçons sur la psychanalyse* (1909), Paris, Payot, coll. " Petite bibliothèque Payot ", 1986, first lesson.

41. See for example the case of Sabina Spielrein, a hysteric beaten as a child by her father, an event that definitively marked her sexuality. She was treated by Jung and then Freud; this story is told in the film by CRONENBERG (David), *A Dangerous Method* (2011).

that this way of making one's interiority visible can be compared to the work of artists[42].

Let us apply this valuable knowledge of modern psychiatry to our clinical case.

Many facts coincide very strangely. Muhammad seems to have suffered a great deal during his childhood. He had to overcome at least two painful bereavements, at the ages of six and eight, not to mention the shadow cast by an absent father, who was probably desired as an indefinable missing ideal. Most likely, he had to suffer from chronic hunger, in this vast and arid land, especially as a poor orphan. This point would be confirmed by his pathetic insistence on describing in his adult revelations paradise with streams, greenery and abundant drink[43]. In this unfavorable setting, it is not impossible that he was frequently beaten, when one takes into account the shady habits of these rough-handed men. In this context, it is not impossible that he was frequently beaten, given the shady habits of these men. Many major inconveniences were likely to push Muhammad to take refuge in a world of dreams, to the point of cracking his fragile personality in the process of formation.

When he said to Moses: "Do not look at the ephemeral pleasures that we have given to several groups

---

42. See in particular FREUD (Sigmund), *Leçons d'introduction à la psychanalyse* (1916-1917), in *Œuvres complètes. Psychoanalysis*, Paris, PUF, 2000, volume XIV, lesson XXIII, pp. 389-390. See also the connection between art and hysteria, notably in *Totem and Taboo* (1912-1913), in *Œuvres complètes. Psychoanalysis*, Paris, PUF, 2000, tome XI, p. 281.
43. See for example *The Qur'an, op. cit.* p. 669.

of them; this is the setting of the life of this world, destined to experience them"[44], we find something of the symptom of derealization, with the perception of the environment as if it were fictional.

Muhammad, in his crises, showed a high poetry. We can identify here the Freudian motif of art as a hysterical type of expression of inner feelings.

In his revelations there appeared a very curious *us, whenever* Muhammad read the Bible again and God intervened in a story. He said of some Jews who were not pious enough in his eyes, "We have punished them because they broke their covenant, because they did not believe in the Signs of God, because they killed prophets unjustly, and because they said, 'Our hearts are uncircumcised.[45] Throughout the Qur'an, the reader may wonder if this *us* refers to Muhammad and God, or Gabriel and God, or all the past prophets, or God alone, but considered multiple, etc. He explicitly stated that he took up the prophets of the Bible (Abraham, Moses, Elijah, Noah, Jesus, etc.): "I am not an innovator among the prophets"[46] and implied that he was imitating them: "... The Book of Moses was a Guide and a Mercy. But this is a Book confirming the others, written in Arabic [...]" [47]

In accordance with the Freudian conception of hysteria, Muhammad was mimicking... sick people. He imitated the prophets. We saw in our previous

---

44. *Ibid*, Sura XX, "Ta. Ha.", verse 131, p. 394.
45. *Ibid*, p. 119.
46. *Ibid*, verse 9, p. 623.
47. *Ibid*, Sura XLVI, "Al 'Ahaqaf", verse 12, p. 623; Sura XLVI, verse 30, p. 627.

work that Jesus was a megaparanoid who invented laws and entities by mythical projections of his collective unconscious[48]. Muhammad, like a hysteric whose seizure badly imitated epilepsy, only mimicked the prophets in an apparent way. He was content to reproduce their words, without invention, image or new parable. He plagiarized roughly his predecessors on the content (monotheism, mercy, absolute divine knowledge, etc.), and on the form (infinite promises and threats, assertions of certain truth where delirium is complete, etc.).

We touch on the likely diagnosis of these seizures. They would correspond exactly to states of dissociative trance, formerly called "hysterical crises", within the framework of a dissociative disorder of identity. On the one hand, we find psychic symptoms of "hysterical conversion" (a psychological conflict is converted into a bodily dysfunction). They are still called "dissociative symptoms": disorders of the memory, the identity, the conscience and the perception of the environment (here, state of trance with revelations). On the other hand, we discover some physical symptoms of conversion, essentially "vagal" in this case. Vagal discomfort is due to the vagal nerve acting too strongly, which has the function of slowing down the heart, resulting in a critical underfeeding of the brain. The conversions are usually rather neurological: paralysis, anesthesia, blindness. Finally, we find a very "favorable" infantile terrain.

---

48. See JOI (Frédéric), *op. cit.* chapter IV, "La mégaparanoïa de Jésus".

Muhammad's disorder does not appear to be a fake problem or a simulation. He was experiencing these seizures. It took him years to integrate them into his personal life, and two decades to integrate them into his social relationships. Today, a psychiatrist would have helped him to superimpose these two identities into a new unit, and adapt it to his social life. Muhammad did exactly the opposite: he "cured" himself, trying to impose his intruding identity on all his people... and succeeded. Such was his disastrous feat. He forced his contemporaries to admit that he was a prophet, the "messenger of God" as he called himself.

Our investigation is progressing. Like that hallucinated angel in his childhood, we hope to have opened Muhammad's heart. Nevertheless, new questions immediately arise. With such a psychological handicap, such a serious and rare disease, how could he convince anyone? *A fortiori*, how could an individual, split into two identities, unify the Arab world, itself so divided? How could he accommodate his people to his intruding identity, instead of adapting it to himself and his society?

If we have glimpsed the heart of Islam, we must also understand how it was able to unfold, first through a recalcitrant Muhammad himself, then in the social fabric of the time, even more reluctant to the words of this strange Gabriel, addressed to a ventriloquist.

CHAPTER TWO
THE VINDICTIVENESS OF MUHAMMAD

Jesus was very aggressive[49], but looks like a choirboy next to Muhammad.

From the outset, he belonged to an aggressive people: "Arab society... had nothing against war and murder, and was very lenient towards the means of war and murder."[50] It was with remarkable ease that he surpassed his contemporaries, coming to power as a "supreme and absolute leader" at the head of a "politico-religious" party, "with a totalitarian vocation"[51] says Maxime Rodinson.

Muhammad's speech contained mostly vindictive messages. The emphasis on love and forgiveness of Jesus had disappeared. Muhammad urged "goodness" but did not elaborate on its content, as if it were self-evident.

---

49. See JOI (Frédéric), *op. cit.* chapter III, "La paranoïa de Jésus", pp. 47-60.
50. RODINSON (Maxime), *op. cit.* p. 250.
51. *Ibid,* p. 249.

Aggression undoubtedly begins with a good dose of hatred, and if possible at an early age. Muhammad writes of his own childhood: "I hated the idols of the Quraysh at an early age, as I hated poetry.[52] After a difficult childhood, Muhammad seemed to keep this grudge against his own clan all his life[53]. He had "hatred".

This was expressed in a feeling of superiority, accompanied by proud condescension, proud disdain and presumptuous contempt. He could declare without embarrassment: "...I know of no young Arab who announces to his people such good news as I do."[54] He looked down on the unconverted: "They are pagans. Their blood is not worth more than the blood of a dog."[55] His condescension was tinged with pretentiousness: "In what condition, tell me, were you when I came to you? You were in darkness and God enlightened you; you were in poverty and God enriched you; you were tearing each other apart and God calmed your hearts." [56]

This haughty aggressiveness also manifested itself in a sexism that has remained attached to the Muslim world. Let us quote a passage among many others, concerning the famous veil: "Tell the believing

---

52. HUSSEIN (Mahmoud), *op. cit.* volume I, p. 206.
53. See also HICHÂM (Ibn), *op. cit.* p. 352; RODINSON (Maxime), *op. cit.* p. 113.
54. HUSSEIN (Mahmoud), *op. cit.* volume I, p. 346.
55. HICHÂM (Ibn), *op. cit.* p. 308.
56. HICHÂM (Ibn), *op. cit.* pp. 235, 290, 364 and 383; *The Qur'an, op. cit.* pp. 762 and 767; HUSSEIN (Mahmud), *op. cit.* volume I, pp. 327 and 390.

women: to lower their gaze, to be chaste, to show only the outside of their finery, to fold their veils over their breasts, to show their finery only to their husbands [...]"[57]. What about the status of woman-object obviously reserved for the woman in paradise, in which... "there will be good and beautiful virgins"[58]. On earth, their share of the inheritance "[...] was half that of the males"[59]. And the Caesar of sexism goes to: "Women] must not do anything seriously shameful. If they do, God gives you permission to quarantine them and to beat them, without too much excess. [Beware, treat your wives well, for they are like prisoners in your house who have nothing of their own. They are only a deposit that God has entrusted to you" [60]

Muhammad's vindictiveness was still expressed in the condemnation of multiple deities, so much so that a delegation of Quraysh notables came to complain to his uncle: "Abû Tâlib, your nephew has insulted our deities, condemned our religion and accused our ancestors of error. Let him stop this provocation [...]"[61] He was always criticizing others, such as Christians[62], Jews[63], speculators[64], the rich[65], or behaviors, such as

---

57. See *The Qur'an, op. cit.* p. 434; but also pp. 286, 439 and 523.
58. *Ibid*, p. 667.
59. RODINSON (Maxime), *op. cit.* p. 267.
60. HICHÂM (Ibn), *op. cit.* p. 397.
61. *Ibid*, pp. 89 and 102; HUSSEIN (Mahmoud), *op. cit.* volume I, pp. 354, 357 and 384.
62. See in particular *The Koran, op. cit.* pp. 228 and 380.
63. RODINSON (Maxime), *op. cit.* p. 231.
64. See in particular *Le Coran, op. cit.* p. 229.
65. See in particular RODINSON (Maxime), *op. cit.* p. 109.

vanity[66], respect for tradition[67], the quest for money and sex[68], morality[69], etc.

We had noted in the mouth of Jesus a nice series of insults[70]. In this respect, we cannot deny Muhammad his proclaimed fidelity to the Bible, he who revived the fashion with his own words. To the unbelievers he would say a very simple "How stupid you are![71] We also find a sentence that would be "amusing", because of the contradiction between its moralizing form and its immoral content, if it were not addressed to Jews surrounded by his troops: "Brothers of the apes and swine, idol worshippers, do you insult me?"[72] We offer a small anthology of these insults exclusively: "They understand nothing"[73], "God knows, and you don't know"[74], "ignorant"[75], "[...] who do not reason"[76], "you think little! "[77], "Father of ignorance" for a man called "Father of wisdom" by his contemporaries[78], "liars"[79],

---

66. See in particular *Le Coran, op. cit.* p. 219.

67. *Ibid,* p. 606.

68. *Ibid,* p. 717.

69. *Ibid,* p. 754.

70. See JOI (Frédéric), *op. cit.* pp. 55-56.

71. *The Qur'an, op. cit,* Sura XL, verse 62, p. 505. See also p. 696.

72. HUSSEIN (Mahmoud), *op. cit.* volume II, p. 349.

73. *The Qur'an, op. cit.* pp. 31, 78, 208 and 238.

74. *Ibid,* pp. 41 and 209.

75. *Ibid,* pp. 168, 268 and 647; HUSSEIN (Mahmoud), *op. cit.* volume I, p. 482.

76. *The Koran, op. cit.* p. 685.

77. *Ibid,* pp. 179 and 715.

78. HUSSEIN (Mahmoud), *op. cit.* volume I, p. 353.

79. *The Koran, op. cit.* pp. 427 and 647.

"fickle"[80], "ungrateful"[81], "their hearts are sick"[82], "they are losing their minds"[83], "perverts"[84], "fools"[85], "abject apes"[86], "dog-like"[87], "the worst of beasts"[88].

As everyone knows, aggressiveness can also turn into mustard, which so often got up Muhammad's nose[89]. Here is an example, in the form of a comical scene:

"Muhammad, if God designed the Creation, who designed God?

At these words, the Messenger of God became so angry that his face changed color. He spoke to them violently. But Gabriel came down and said to him:

- Keep calm, Muhammad.

Then he gave him God's answer:

- Say: He is God the One, God who is by Himself, who does not beget, who is not begotten, and of whom no one is equal.

After the Messenger of God had recited to the people the verse that Gabriel had just conveyed to him, they said to him:

- Well, Muhammad, describe him to us. What is his face like? How are his arms, his forearms...

---

80. *Ibid*, p. 509.
81. *Ibid.*
82. *Ibid*, p. 219.
83. *Ibid*, p. 5.
84. *Ibid,* pp. 19, 71, 76 and 195.
85. *Ibid.* at 25 and 647.
86. *Ibid*, p. 13.
87. *Ibid*, p. 208.
88. *Ibid*, p. 215.
89. See in particular HICHÂM (Ibn), *op. cit.* pp. 121, 228 and 406; HUSSEIN (Mahmud), *op. cit.* volume II, pp. 60, 83 and 103.

At these words, the Messenger of God became even more angry than before. Then Gabriel came back and told him again that he should keep calm [...] " [90]

Let's go a little further to the dark side of force, passing from anger to threat: "Listen to me, men of the Quraysh, I bring the sword by which you will die by slitting your throats, I swear by Him who holds my life in His hand."[91] If death was not enough, threats were made against the unfortunate offenders after life[92]. The Qur'an, which according to its modest author is "the most beautiful of stories"[93], is full of delicious details about the future promised to the recalcitrant: "Announce a painful punishment to those who hoard gold and silver without spending anything in the way of God, on the day when these metals will be brought to incandescence in the Fire of Gehenna and will serve to mark their foreheads, their flanks and their backs: 'This is what you hoarded; taste what you hoarded!'"[94], " [...] those who will be drunk with boiling water that will tear their entrails [...] "[95], " here is an inferno: it tears off the members [...] "[96]. During his attacks, he had hallucinations of rare violence. When he sought

---

90. *Ibid. in* Volume II, p. 71.
91. HICHÂM (Ibn), *op. cit.* pp. 96, 227 and 273; *Le Coran, op. cit.* pp. 10, 56 and 125; HUSSEIN (Mahmoud), *op. cit.* volume I, pp. 355 and 466, volume II, p. 357; RODINSON (Maxime), *op. cit.* p. 225.
92. *The Qur'an, op. cit.* pp. 4, 5, 7, 16, 17, 19, 20, 28, 30, 36, 37, 56, 63, 87, 93, 102, 194, 209, 266, 347, 616, 618, 635, 646, 651, 704, 716, 718, 731 and 740.
93. *Ibid,* p. 569.
94. *Ibid,* p. 229.
95. *Ibid.* at 630.
96. *Ibid,* p. 716.

an infernal punishment for women who had given their husbands children conceived with other men, he imagined "women hanging by their breasts"[97]. No doubt he was preparing the manual of the perfect inquisitor.

The much more subtle and insidious reverse side of these threats consisted of absolutely untenable promises, in the straight line of Jesus[98]. Aggression was expressed as a desire for control, since promises are only binding on those who receive them. Muhammad, if he did not invent this stratagem, added a few touches of his own, which make us smile, so much so that we can see the relativism of his personal geographical situation and his own taste for young women: "The companions of the right will stand among thornless jujube trees and acacia trees in a row. They will enjoy ample shade, running water, and abundant fruit that is neither picked in advance nor forbidden. They will rest on high beds. Verily, it is We Who have created the Houris in a perfect way. We have made them virgins, loving and of equal youth for the companions of the right.[99] Muhammad kept promising, without incurring any cost, wealth, immortality, erasure of faults, happiness, paradise, not to mention rain, rivers and even a river[100].

---

97. HICHÂM (Ibn), *op. cit.* p. 146.
98. JOI (Frédéric), *op. cit.* pp. 53-55.
99. *The Koran, op. cit.* p. 669.
100. *Ibid.* including pp. 4, 7, 13, 16, 36, 53, 63, 80, 90, 94, 100, 102, 109, 178, 199, 244, 245, 272, 360, 518, 550, 611, 616, 629, 630, 637, 639, 642, 652, 669 and 738.

Muhammad's vindictiveness was still manifested in his extremely authoritarian character. As a tyrannical Zeus, he brought down the thunderbolt of laws and orders on his contemporaries. "...] Muhammad ordered his companions and other Muslims to flee to Medina and join their brothers the Ançâr"[101]. He forced the Banû Qaynuqâ' into exile[102]. To his followers, "he ordered them to attack in the name of God"[103]. "During the battle of Khaybar, the Prophet forbade the Muslims four things: He forbade them to eat the meat of domestic donkeys. He forbade them to eat donkey meat. This prohibition came at the time when the pots full of donkey meat were boiling. [He forbade them to eat any wild animal with fangs. Thirdly, he forbade them to go near pregnant captives, so as not to water what another had sown. Finally, he forbade them to appropriate or sell any booty before the final distribution."[104] As a final mark of authority, even though Muhammad "never refused anything to his wife"[105], his own wives eventually obeyed his orders: "The threat of general repudiation [...] was effective. The women had lost the taste for contradicting the Prophet so valiantly supported by his god. They let him do as he pleased.[106] Generally speaking,

---

101. HICHÂM (Ibn), *op. cit.* p. 163.
102. HUSSEIN (Mahmoud), *op. cit.* volume II, p. 198.
103. HICHÂM (Ibn), *op. cit.* p. 312.
104. *Ibid*, pp. 312-313.
105. *Ibid*, p. 217.
106. RODINSON (Maxime), *op. cit.* p. 320.

Muhammad used the imperative very commonly to conjugate his verbs[107].

Muhammad was very keen to see his people "subjugated"[108], for example by declaring himself the leader[109] or by calling disobedience of his own laws "blasphemy"[110]. "Who, then, keeps his pact better than God? [Those who return to God, those who worship him, those who praise him, those who engage in exercises of piety, those who bow down, those who prostrate themselves, those who command what is proper, those who forbid what is blameworthy, those who observe the laws of God....".[111] We understand why *submitted* is said in Arabic *moslim* in the singular, *moslimoun* in the plural (hence *Muslim*). *Submission* derives from the infinitive of the same word, *islâm*[112]. "Religion, in the eyes of God, is truly Submission.[113] Just as Jesus rightly called his listeners "sheep," we will call the gullible followers of Muhammad "submissives" - pejorative words for democratic Westerners who rely on the rational choices of individuals. This system of absolute orders of supposedly divine origin led to a

---

107. See his authoritarian orders in: HICHÂM (Ibn), *op. cit.* pp. 112, 188, 319, 390 and 404; HUSSEIN (Mahmud), *op. cit.* volume I, pp. 271, 354 and 528; volume II, p. 155; *The Qur'an, op. cit.* pp. 6, 9, 21, 27, 34, 35, 42, 47, 107, 111, 177, 211, 335, 631 and 710.
108. *Ibid*, pp. 7, 13, 16, 32, 103, 334, 402, 680, 684, 710 and 748; HICHÂM (Ibn), *op. cit.* p. 182; HUSSEIN (Mahmoud), *op. cit.*
109. *Ibid. in* Volume II, p. 48.
110. See in particular HUSSEIN (Mahmoud), *op. cit.* volume II, p. 99.
111. *The Koran, op. cit.* p. 243.
112. RODINSON (Maxime), *op. cit.* p. 221.
113. *The Koran, op. cit.* p. 62.

theocracy. The faithful Abû Bakr, the first caliph after Muhammad's death, was able to rely on this authority to reproduce the same tyrannical relationship established by his master with his submissives: "As long as I obey God and his Prophet, obey me; and if I disobey God and his Prophet, I will no longer be entitled to your obedience. Get up for prayer. God save you!"[114] To obtain this submission, Muhammad used the good old political means of dividing his enemies or even their families to better rule[115].

He also spent a great deal of time righting wrongs of all kinds[116]. He went so far as to reproach the Jews for their ignorance, who could not believe their ears, so much did he draw all his inspiration from their Torah:

"It has come to our attention that you said, "You have received little knowledge. Is it to us that you intended these words?

- Yes, it's yours." [117]

His aggressiveness was further expressed in the excessive demands he often made[118] : "Many of the companions prayed sitting down, so high was their fever. The Messenger of God went to them and said, "Know that sitting prayer is worth half as much as standing prayer." So, despite their weakness and the

---

114. HICHÂM (Ibn), *op. cit.* p. 413.
115. See especially *The Koran, op. cit.* pp. 175, 212 and 227.
116. HUSSEIN (Mahmoud), *op. cit.* volume II, pp. 42, 43, 55, 291, 310 and 375; *The Koran, op. cit.* pp. 20, 21, 606, 677 and 693.
117. HUSSEIN (Mahmoud), *op. cit.* volume II, p. 57.
118. *Ibid,* vol. II, pp. 92, 144 and 374; *The Qur'an, op. cit,* pp. 230 and 588.

suffering they endured, they made the effort to stand up to earn divine favor." [119]

Muhammad was also intolerant: "...the last recommendation of the Prophet was: 'There must be only one religion in the island of the Arabs.[120] This intransigence naturally degenerated into communitarianism and racism, which appear in many passages: "Do not take the Jews and Christians for friends." [121]

We move imperceptibly to the dark side of power, from words to deeds. Already at this stage, Muhammad was the cause of quarrels, fights and family rifts[122]. The first drop of blood was soon shed in his name[123]. As with Jesus[124], Muhammad was clearly reaping the fruits of his own aggression[125]. From the time of his first revelations, when the inner voice ordered him to warn those closest to him, Muhammad "feared that the task was beyond his strength, for it could not fail to provoke the resentment of those closest to him"[126]. He insulted their gods and said that their fathers, who had died in error, were burning in the fires of Hell. This provoked

---

119. HUSSEIN (Mahmoud), *op. cit.* volume II, p. 36.
120. HICHÂM (Ibn), *op. cit.* pp. 415, 149 and 322. See also *The Koran, op. cit.* pp. 228 and 692.
121. *Ibid,* pp. 135, 430 and 691; HUSSEIN (Mahmud), *op. cit.* volume II, p. 80. The Jews expelled from Medina: Rodinson (Maxime), *op. cit.* p. 226.
122. *Ibid,* pp. 137 and 205; HICHÂM (Ibn), *op. cit,* pp. 90, 91, 109, 122, 123, 124, 152, 164, 165, 172 and 218; HUSSEIN (Mahmud), *op. cit,* vol. I, pp. 330, 345, 347, 351, 358, 386, 391, 405, 432, 443, 444, 448, 470, 474 and 478, and vol.
123. HICHÂM (Ibn), *op. cit.* p. 89.
124. See JOI (Frédéric), *op. cit.* pp. 81-89. ·
125. See HICHÂM (Ibn), *op. cit.,* pp. 95-96.
126. HUSSEIN (Mahmoud), *op. cit.* volume I, p. 343.

the fury of the Meccans"[127]. "The word of Muhammad is indeed a spell, by means of which he breaks the bonds between son and father, between husband and wife, between brother and brother, between members of the same tribe"[128]. As Ibn Hichâm notes: "In sum, on the eve of the Hegira, the Yathribins and the Meccans knew each other quite well. Their relations were friendly commercial, rather competitive, but never conflicting. The arrival of Muhammad with his prophetic mission will gradually and radically change these relations.[129] And for good reason: they would come to declare war on each other.

A little anecdote: Muhammad allowed himself to blackmail God at least once, in order to win a battle: "He said, among other prayers: "If my companions perish today, Lord, you will not be worshipped." [130]

Let us now examine a very dark trait of the father of Islam: an immeasurable grudge against all those who doubted his message, mocked him or put obstacles in his way, especially in the political arena[131]. He was particularly angry with his own clan, whose hostility had forced him to flee Mecca for Medina. He even spoke to the corpses of the Quraysh after a battle, even though his grudge had been satisfied: "You have

---

127. *Ibid*, p. 348.
128. *Ibid*, p. 385.
129. HICHÂM (Ibn), *op. cit.* p. 171.
130. *Ibid*, p. 203.
131. *Ibid*, pp. 124, 125, 191, 220, 258, 332 and 339; *The Qur'an, op. cit*, pp. 239, 269, 400, 558, 574, 618 and 621; HUSSEIN (Mahmoud), *op. cit*, vol. I, pp. 470 and 478, vol. II, pp. 48, 77 and 284; RODINSON (Maxime), *op. cit,* p. 194.

not respected the tribal bond between you and the Prophet from your own tribe. You called me a liar while others believed me; you exiled me and others welcomed me; you fought me and others supported me."[132] Muhammad never forgot the offenses he suffered. 'Ubqa ibn Abû Mu'ît had spat in his face and on another occasion had dumped a bag of filth on his shoulders during a prayer at the Mosque. When the opportunity arose, many years later, Muhammad had him beheaded[133]. Al-Nadr ibn al-Harith had been making fun of Muhammad for years before the Hegira. He claimed to be able to tell more beautiful and worthwhile stories than he could. Years later, Muhammad would do the same to him[134]. The former scribe of his revelations, 'Abdallah ibn Sa'd, who had left him because he realized that phrases of his own could be endorsed by Muhammad, incurred the wrath of his resentment for years. His younger brother, 'Uthman, asked for the pardon of this man who represented what the sowers of ideologies hate the most: lucid rational criticism. 'Uthman insisted so much that the Prophet finally gave in, but then he said to those present, "I have been silent for a long time. Why didn't one of you kill that dog?[135] Such examples are legion, especially with the poets who had mocked him[136]. Muhammad was so resentful that his conception of God was clearly affected by it, contrary to the

---

132. HICHÂM (Ibn), *op. cit.* p. 210.
133. HUSSEIN (Mahmoud), *op. cit.* volume II, pp. 164-165.
134. *Ibid. in* Volume II, pp. 165-166.
135. RODINSON (Maxime), *op. cit.* p. 297.
136. HICHÂM (Ibn), *op. cit.* p. 366.

Christian tradition which he claimed to prolong: "God is powerful, he is the Master of vengeance."[137] He dreamed, through his interposed god, of absolute revenge: "The Day when the earth will be replaced by another earth, when the heavens will be replaced by other heavens. Men will then be presented to God, the One, the Supreme Dominator! On that Day, you will see the guilty chained two by two. Their tunics will be made of tar; fire will cover their faces."[138] The following anecdote adds to this the absence of mercy: "... his resentment was unleashed against two men who had directed intellectual attacks against him. They had inquired of Jewish and Iranian sources, had asked him difficult questions. They had mocked him and his divine messages. They had no forgiveness to expect. He ordered them to be executed. One of them said to him, "And who will take care of my boys, Mohammad?" He replied, "Hell!" " [139]

With such an aggressive nature, no one will be surprised to learn that Muhammad was frightening[140], nor that he made his relatives feel guilty[141].

Before going into the many examples of black acts, let us take the trouble to point out an important fact. Muhammad took over the split from Jesus, concerning

---

137. *The Koran, op. cit.* p. 60. See also pp. 634 and 696, for example.
138. *Ibid*, pp. 314-315.
139. RODINSON (Maxime), *op. cit.* p. 200.
140. HICHÂM (Ibn), *op. cit.* pp. 96, 136 and 230; RODINSON (Maxime), *op. cit.* p. 203; HUSSEIN (Mahmoud), *op. cit.* volume II, p. 165.
141. *The Koran, op. cit.* p. 545.

his own community[142]. In effect, he dispensed rewards, love, happiness, etc., to those who obeyed him, and reserved all the violence of his aggression for others. This contradictory treatment went so far as to divide Jews and Christians into "good" and "bad" depending on whether they were applying the Bible correctly or incorrectly (his own interpretation of it)[143] : they either believed "correctly" or "incorrectly". Like Jesus, he was extremely demanding and castigated the slightest laxity in belief[144]. This led to the unbelievable situation that the rules of goodness only applied within the Umma, which implied the right to unleash aggression, to steal, to kill, to rape, etc., outside! "Man should therefore believe in Allah and his Prophet, practice good, that is, what Allah has commanded, and avoid evil, that is, what Allah has forbidden. He should be generous, kind, benevolent, respectful to his parents, honest, polite, just, abstain from murder and theft as well as from fornication, i.e. unauthorized sexual relations, and observe the dietary prohibitions. He should show a spirit of solidarity within the community."[145] In short: benevolence within, war on others[146]. Islam needed enemies to vent its aggression on the outside, just as states do in times of crisis and dictatorships do at all times.

---

142. See in particular JOI (Frédéric), *op. cit.* pp. 120-121.
143. *The Koran, op. cit.* pp. 138-139.
144. See JOI (Frédéric), *op. cit.* pp. 73-74.
145. RODINSON (Maxime), *op. cit.* pp. 281-282.
146. See in particular *Le Coran, op. cit.* pp. 222 and 640; HUSSEIN (Mahmoud), *op. cit.* volume II, pp. 47-48; RODINSON (Maxime), *op. cit.* pp. 183, 185, 187, 238 and 263.

To begin with violence, it is well known that Muhammad encouraged corporal punishment: "Hit the debauchee and the debauchee with a hundred lashes each. Do not be lenient with them in order to respect the religion of God... a group of believers will witness their punishment.[147] Concerning women: "Admonish those whose infidelity you fear; relegate them to separate rooms and strike them."[148] "Cut off the hands of the thief and the thiefess [...]"[149] He encouraged stoning, which he required to be applied on some occasions[150]. On other occasions, he ordered the destruction of idols[151] and sacred places[152].

His most odious directives concerned murder[153], and were often carried out[154]. These commissioned assassinations served his political purposes by targeting his opponents, as a worthy dictator would[155]. In a very cynical way, he went so far as to have a prisoner of war murdered in order to marry his beautiful young wife, violating in the process his own prohibition

---

147. *The Koran, op. cit.* p. 430. For the whip, see also HICHAM (Ibn), *op. cit.* p. 298.
148. *Ibid,* p. 99.
149. *Ibid,* p. 132.
150. See in particular HUSSEIN (Mahmoud), *op. cit.* volume I, p. 25; volume II, pp. 62 and 403.
151. HUSSEIN (Mahmoud), *op. cit.* volume I, p. 329.
152. HICHÂM (Ibn), *op. cit.* p. 372.
153. See in particular HICHÂM (Ibn), *op. cit.* pp. 212, 230, 282 and 288; *Le Coran, op. cit.* pp. 36, 647, 696 and 771; HUSSEIN (Mahmoud), *op. cit.* volume I, p. 428; volume II, pp. 258, 271, 276 and 358; RODINSON (Maxime), *op. cit.* p. 203.
154. See in particular HUSSEIN (Mahmoud), *op. cit.* volume II, p. 275; RODINSON (Maxime), *op. cit.* p. 229.
155. *Ibid,* p. 189.

against marrying a captive before the end of her menstrual period[156]. During a hallucination, a mysterious traveler gave him the mission to decapitate his own[157]. He went so far as to order a genocide: "The Prophet recommended to his companions: 'Any Jew who falls into your hands, kill him.'" So when the Prophet prevailed over the Jews of the Banû Quraydha, he took nearly four hundred prisoners and gave orders to slit their throats."[158]

On many occasions[159], Muhammad heavily implied that killing is right in some cases, in the name of God of course: "Do not kill anyone unjustly, God forbids it."[160]

Very often, what remained only wishes for revenge were followed by real actions[161]. One day, he insisted several times on eliminating a poet who had simply offended him, and even allowed a divine prohibition to be broken in order to cowardly surprise his target:

"The Messenger of God then said:

- Deliver me from Ka'b ibn al-Ashraf, and from the poems he composes and goes around reciting. Who will take care of this man who wrongs me? [...]

- To succeed in killing this man, we ask your permission to lie.

---

156. *Ibid*, p. 289; HICHÂM (Ibn), *op. cit.* p. 401.
157. HUSSEIN (Mahmoud), *op. cit.* volume I, p. 286.
158. HICHÂM (Ibn), *op. cit.* p. 232.
159. *Ibid*, pp. 169, 344 and 476; *The Qur'an, op. cit.* p. 183; HUSSEIN (Mahmoud), *op. cit.* volume I, p. 48.
160. *Ibid. in* Volume I, p. 480.
161. RODINSON (Maxime), *op. cit.* pp. 286, 298, 366 and 405; *Le Coran, op. cit.* p. 36; HUSSEIN (Mahmoud), *op. cit.* volume II, pp. 164-165; RODINSON (Maxime), *op. cit.* p. 200.

The Messenger of God replied:

- Do." [162]

More prosaically, Muhammad wished to behead[163] : "By Him who holds the soul of Muhammad in His hands, I have a mission to cut off heads." [164]

He had an undeniable sadism[165]. He enjoyed seeing a decapitated head[166], watching the war[167] or hearing the names of the Quraysh dead after a battle[168]. He took the kettledrum when his uncle Abû Tâlib was dying and asked his rich nephew for some medicine from heaven to relieve him. It was not much to ask. This relative had adopted him at the age of eight, educated him for a long time and then protected him from the Quraysh after the revelations. His only fault was that he refused to convert. The ungrateful nephew's reply was scathing, and twice: "God has forbidden the disbelievers any food or drink from Paradise." [169]

Muhammad used torture cheerfully[170], especially on "prisoners to serve as an example"[171].

162. HUSSEIN (Mahmoud), *op. cit.* volume II, pp. 202-203.

163. HICHÂM (Ibn), *op. cit.* p. 385.

164. HUSSEIN (Mahmoud), *op. cit.* volume I, p. 444.

165. See especially *The Qur'an, op. cit.* pp. 247, 410 and 739.

166. RODINSON (Maxime), *op. cit.* p. 222.

167. HICHÂM (Ibn), *op. cit.* p. 351.

168. HUSSEIN (Mahmoud), *op. cit.* volume II, p. 160.

169. *Ibid,* volume I, p. 416. On the death of Abû Tâlib, see pp. 415-419, in particular the final note of the commentator, p. 419.

170. HICHÂM (Ibn), *op. cit.* pp. 197, 206 and 317.

171. RODINSON (Maxime), *op. cit.* p. 284.

The dark crescendo to horror continues with a very clear encouragement to raids, battles and war[172]. We find in the Koran an ancestral form of what we would call today mental "coaching", through trust[173]. Maxime Rodinson finely analyzes the passage from the first razzias, which served both as an outlet and a source of income for the Meccan exiles in Medina, to battles between Arabs, to external wars: "As Arabia adhered in one form or another to this peaceful system [within the 'Umma], the traditional resource of razzia at the expense of enemy tribes dried up. The men, for whom the small permanent war between rival groups represented the virile occupation par excellence, became idle, feeling as if they were emasculated. Arabia had too many men and not enough arable land to feed its inhabitants. Agriculture was a despised profession. The only solution was to turn the warlike energy of the Arabs against the civilized and agricultural countries on the edge of the desert, against that Fertile Crescent which belonged partly to the Byzantine Empire, partly to the Sassanid Persian Empire."[174] "The Arabs had many times before attacked the sedentary peoples of the Fertile Crescent."[175] For all intents and purposes, let us recall the definition of a parasite: an animal or plant organism that lives at the expense of another

---

172. HICHÂM (Ibn), *op. cit.* p. 163; *Le Coran, op. cit.* pp. 79, 104, 105, 214, 221, 224, 229, 239, 245, 321, 322, 633, 691 and 692; HUSSEIN (Mahmoud), *op. cit.* volume II, p. 225; RODINSON (Maxime), *op. cit.* p. 205.
173. *The Qur'an, op. cit.* pp. 84, 231 and 516.
174. RODINSON (Maxime), *op. cit.* p. 310.
175. *Ibid*, p. 332.

organism, to which it causes more or less serious damage, without however destroying it. Let's also remember that agriculture was a revolutionary step in the long history of humanity, which made it possible to pass from the Paleolithic to the Neolithic, nearly ten thousand years ago.

If we summarize this dark journey, the local aggressiveness of an individual was such that it ended up setting a whole region, and later a vast geographical area, not to say the whole world, ablaze. Spilling one's overflow of aggression outside is never more than a very unstable and temporary solution that inevitably leads to a tragic flight forward.

To complete this account of Muhammad's vindictiveness, we should note that he himself had a hand in not only a battle[176], but also in the genocide of the Banû Quraydha: "The prophet did not cease to slit their throats until they were totally exterminated.[177] Wouldn't today's Americans see in this an ancestor of the *serial killer*?

It will be retorted that he tried to convert them... Let us add: by force[178]. Is it necessary to specify that "to convert by force" appears as a contradiction in terms? Let us admire the work of Muhammad: Say: "There is no god but God! And you will safeguard your lives and your property."[179]

---

176. *Ibid*, p. 213.
177. HICHÂM (Ibn), *op. cit.* p. 277.
178. *Ibid*, pp. 68 and 392; *The Qur'an, op. cit.* pp. 36 and 301; HUSSEIN (Mahmud), *op. cit.* volume II, pp. 15 and 65.
179. *Ibid. in* Volume II, p. 382.

In desperation with these Jews, Muhammad "... ordered to kill all the men of the Banû Quraydha, and even the young ones, from the age when they had the hair of puberty"[180]. Let us also note this variant, for the sake of finesse: "I order that all men of shaving age be put to death, that women and children be enslaved and that their property be divided among the Muslims", a judgment that Muhammad considered in conformity with that of God[181]. This was the beginning of Muhammad's genocide[182]: "The next day he had large pits dug in the market of Medina. The next day, he had the Jews tied up in bundles and beheaded one by one at the edge of the pits and threw them in. Some say there were six or seven hundred of them, others say eight or nine hundred. [183]

On the psychological level, we can only observe this uncontrolled bubbling of aggressiveness and violence. On the philosophical level, we do not condemn aggressiveness in itself, as it is necessary for the survival of a species[184]. Nor do we approve of the Christian idea of fighting aggression with love. If this mechanism worked, the mawkish sentimentality of Americans would have long since overcome their mania for mass murder. Christianity seriously misunderstands the unconscious intertwining of love and hate impulses. For reasons of logic, fighting aggression

---

180. HICHÂM (Ibn), *op. cit.* p. 277.
181. HUSSEIN (Mahmoud), *op. cit.* volume II, p. 356.
182. *Ibid. in* Volume II, p. 18.
183. RODINSON (Maxime), *op. cit.* p. 247.
184. See in particular LORENZ (Konrad), *L'Agression*, Paris, Flammarion, 1983, chapter III, "À quoi le monde est-il bon?"

with aggression would not be appropriate either. And once again, to wish to eliminate aggressiveness remains a nonsense: "*To remove* passions and appetites, only to prevent their stupidity or the unfortunate consequences of their stupidity, here is what today seems to us to be only an acute form of stupidity. We no longer admire dentists who *pull out* teeth so that they no longer hurt..."[185] What to do?

The solution to this problem could well be found in two expressions, used by two thinkers: the "spiritualization of passion"[186] or the "sublimation of impulses". We wish that the man sublimates as well his hatred as his love, to rise to the order of the representations, the concepts, the knowledge. The violence represents a not sublimated destiny of the impulse of hate. Alas! It is the main way that Muhammad had chosen to flow his massive aggressiveness. A beautiful dead end.

How could this dark approach survive and become widespread? How could this aggressiveness, rebellious to any order, order the aggressiveness of an entire people? How could the poor abused orphan, suffering from a dissociative disorder and a hatred at the origin of many discords, become rich, adored, powerful, surrounded by women, and... die in peace?

---

185. NIETZSCHE (Friedrich), *Crépuscule des idoles* (1888), in *Œuvres philosophiques complètes*, Paris, Gallimard-NRF, 1990, tome VIII, " La morale, une anti-nature ", § 1, p. 82.
186. *Ibid.*

CHAPTER THREE
THE MEANING OF MUHAMMAD'S ORDER

Like his mentor Jesus[187], Muhammad was a whole person, with a particularly binary worldview and choices[188]. We particularly appreciate the fine nuances of his words: "Men are divided into two groups; on the one hand, the blind and the deaf, on the other hand, the one who sees and the one who hears. Are they comparable? Don't you think?"[189] As Sergio Leone had his characters say in *The Good, the Bad and the Ugly*, "the world is divided into two categories." But that was humorous. Not here: "Bad women to bad men; bad to bad! Those who are good, to those who are good; those who are good, to those who are good!"[190] Although.

For those who are not thinking straight, we strongly recommend reading the Qur'an, which will motivate

---

187. See JOI (Frédéric), *op. cit.* chapter II.
188. See in particular *Le Coran, op. cit.* pp. 118, 135, 145, 206 and 514; HICHÂM (Ibn), *op. cit.* pp. 89, 145 and 149; HUSSEIN (Mahmoud), *op. cit.* volume II, pp. 61 and 386.
189. *The Koran, op. cit.* p. 267.
190. *Ibid*, p. 433.

you with the inspiring example of its author: "Uncle, I swear, if they put the sun in my right hand and the moon in my left hand so that I give up this mission, I will not do it, until God makes the truth come out or I die.[191] For those who are too easily discouraged in the face of adversity, let us suggest yet another challenging model: "When God and His Prophet have made a decision, it is not fitting for a believer, male or female, to maintain his or her choice on that matter."[192] By definition, a man who has pursued his people for twenty years to make them take their hallucinations seriously deserves at least the title of "persevering", at most the title of "king of the obstinate"[193].

When it came to finding a serious man to whom to entrust the high responsibility of placing the sacred stone at the corner of the newly rebuilt Ka'ba shrine, the Meccans chose Muhammad[194]. "He would have been thirty-five years old. He would have been called "al-amîn", that is to say "the sure man", in whom one can trust.[195] Khadijah had chosen Muhammad as her husband and business partner, despite her poverty, because of his loyal, responsible character and his fidelity to his commitments[196]. All his life

---

191. HICHÂM (Ibn), *op. cit.* p. 90.

192. *The Koran, op. cit.* p. 519.

193. *Ibid*, pp. 351, 540 and 645; HICHÂM (Ibn), *op. cit*, pp. 90, 95 and 102; HUSSEIN (Mahmud), *op. cit*, vol. I, pp. 222 (insisting on the age of twelve), 358, 404, 405, 416 and 418.

194. See RODINSON (Maxime), *op. cit.* pp. 76 and 77.

195. *Ibid*, p. 77.

196. See HICHÂM (Ibn), *op. cit.* p. 59; HUSSEIN (Mahmud), *op. cit.* volume I, p. 249.

he confirmed these personality traits[197], which he conveniently made a divine imperative: "Keep your commitments, for men will be questioned about their commitments."[198]

At the time when Muhammad himself feared that he might become a poet or a man possessed, his first wife Khadijah reassured him with these words: "God will not do this to you, knowing what I know of the sincerity of your word, your scrupulous honesty, your high morality and your fidelity to the bonds of kinship."[199] He had indeed a strong sense of duty[200]. His uprightness[201] and his probity[202] were also manifested in his hatred of injustice: "Woe to the fraudsters! When they buy something, they demand full measure from people; when they measure or weigh for them, they cheat."[203] Corruption did not disgust him any less: "Do not devour your possessions wrongly among yourselves; do not make a present of them to the judges for the purpose of eating unjustly a share of another's property."[204]

---

197. See in particular *Le Coran, op. cit.* pp. 33, 124, 142 and 717; HICHÂM (Ibn), *op. cit.* pp. 58, 144, 174, 177, 263 and 309; HUSSEIN (Mahmoud), *op. cit.* volume I, pp. 318, 327 and 515.
198. *The Koran, op. cit.* p. 344.
199. HUSSEIN (Mahmoud), *op. cit.* volume I, p. 311.
200. *Le Coran, op. cit.* pp. 329 and 737; HICHÂM (Ibn), *op. cit.* pp. 58, 175, 235 and 362; HUSSEIN (Mahmoud), *op. cit.* volume II, pp. 40; RODINSON (Maxime), *op. cit.* p. 75.
201. See HUSSEIN (Mahmoud), *op. cit.* volume I, p. 250.
202. *Ibid. in* Volume I, p. 271.
203. *The Koran, op. cit.* p. 745.
204. *Ibid,* p. 35.

In the same vein, Muhammad was very concerned about politeness: "Let your slaves and those of you who have not yet reached puberty ask permission to enter your homes at three times of the day: before the dawn prayer; in the middle of the day, when you remove your clothes; and after the evening prayer."[205]

Muhammad was very particular about the application of the rules: "Give a just measure when you measure; weigh with the most exact scale. This is good, and the result is excellent.[206] He insisted on re-enforcing the letter of an outdated law such as stoning[207].

Like Jesus[208], Muhammad had a keen sense of purity and cleanliness[209] : "When you prepare for prayer, wash your faces and hands up to the elbows; pass your hands over your heads and feet up to the ankles. If you are in a state of legal impurity, purify yourself. If you are sick, or on a journey; if one of you has come from a hidden place; if you have had dealings with women and cannot find water, use good sand and rub it on your faces and hands.[210] This haunting theme carried over to the moral plane: "Without God's grace upon you and his mercy, no one among you would ever be clean."[211] That said, Muhammad's cleanliness remained relative to his people. He was only more

---

205. *Ibid,* p. 439. See also p. 433, as well as HUSSEIN (Mahmoud), *op. cit.* volume I, p. 347, on the lie.
206. *The Koran, op. cit.* p. 344.
207. HUSSEIN (Mahmoud), *op. cit.* volume II, p. 62.
208. JOI (Frédéric), *op. cit.* pp. 39-40.
209. See *Le Coran, op. cit.* pp. 25, 28, 83, 100, 213, 228, 693 and 726; HUSSEIN (Mahmud), *op. cit.* volume II, p. 13.
210. *The Koran, op. cit.* p. 126.
211. *Ibid,* p. 432.

demanding than his contemporaries, whose level of hygiene the reader will judge: "Every Muslim must wash every seventh day, and wash both his head and the rest of his body."[212]

As an amusing transition between his obsession with purity and his taste for money, let us quote a beautiful passage from the Qur'an, which is addressed to those who have done a good deed and a bad one: "Take alms from their property to purify it and make it spotless."[213] In other words, Muhammad found the subtle and dubious way to derive income from the impurity of men - an inexhaustible source!

Muhammad was venal[214]. Before battles, his prayers went up to God only to come down to earth: "I hope God will give us their goods as booty.[215] After the battles, he would get back, by divine decree of course, a fifth of the booty[216]. But not always..." As for the booty of Fadak, it went entirely to the Prophet, because God had sown terror in the hearts of its inhabitants, when they learned of the fate reserved for the Jews of Khaybar. They made peace with the Prophet without fighting, leaving him half of their property.[217] If this was not enough, Muhammad had some other source of income: "[...] the Prophet sent emissaries

---

212. HUSSEIN (Mahmoud), *op. cit.* volume II, p. 89.
213. *The Koran, op. cit.* p. 241.
214. *Ibid,* pp. 212, 218 and 726; HICHÂM (Ibn), *op. cit.* p. 318; HUSSEIN (Mahmoud), *op. cit.* volume II, pp. 107, 302 and 303; RODINSON (Maxime), *op. cit.* pp. 227, 259 and 260.
215. HUSSEIN (Mahmoud), *op. cit.* volume II, p. 383.
216. See in particular HICHÂM (Ibn), *op. cit.* p. 322; HUSSEIN (Mahmud), *op. cit.* volume II, p. 167.
217. HICHÂM (Ibn), *op. cit.* p. 322.

and officials wherever Islam had taken hold, in order to collect donations from the faithful "[218]. Muhammad thus enriched himself from theft, fear and belief. The money he "collected" was supposed to serve this kind of nascent state, but its functioning is strangely reminiscent of those African countries where international aid is equivalent to the private fortune of the "president", since "the public treasury was not distinguished from Muhammad's personal fortune"[219].

Some rich people like to count their money. Muhammad often used accounting terms[220]. He was very meticulous, and this is reflected in the attributes he gives to God: "We shall set up the exact scales on the Day of Judgment. No man shall be wronged for the smallest thing; if it were the weight of a mustard seed, we would bring it. We are enough to do the counting.[221] After his first life as a merchant, "his language will always be peppered with commercial locutions"[222].

Muhammad was adept at calculating interests[223]. Already his first marriage was an advantageous calculation to get out of his miserable situation[224]. It was not the last one concluded for political purposes[225]. He still proceeded thus in battles: "War, 'Umar, is a matter

---

218. *Ibid*, p. 394.
219. *Ibid*, p. 259.
220. *The Qur'an, op. cit.* pp. 38, 218 and 381.
221. *Ibid*, pp. 400-401.
222. RODINSON (Maxime), *op. cit.* p. 76.
223. *The Koran, op. cit.* pp. 600-700; HICHÂM (Ibn), *op. cit.* pp. 155-216; HUSSEIN (Mahmud), *op. cit.* volume I, pp. 386-502.
224. RODINSON (Maxime), *op. cit.* pp. 74-75.
225. *Ibid*, p. 317.

of cunning.[226] Maxime Rodinson still sees him as a great political calculator[227], especially in the "good" use of murders[228], strategic massacres[229], or in the art of war[230]. This author writes: "Mohammad knew how to buy influential people with appropriate gifts, to play in true politics with ambition, greed, vanity, fear, and sometimes no doubt (but much more rarely) with men's appetite for ideals and devotion."[231] Other passages attest to this aspect of intrigue in politics[232].

In general, Muhammad tended to intellectualize, to seek interest, to calculate his actions. In this sense, he tried to control his own emotions and often remained impassive[233]. Certainly, he had to take a lot of trouble with regard to his ebullient temperament. But this organized character allowed him to make political calculation prevail over anger when his long-term interest was at stake[234]. It is still in this sense that he was able to show himself incorruptible, the high consideration of his "mission" took precedence over his greed: "Nephew, if by your message you aim at fortune, we will give you of our wealth, enough to be

226. HUSSEIN (Mahmud), *op. cit.* volume I, p. 337; *The Koran, op. cit.* p. 286; HICHÂM (Ibn), *op. cit.* p. 268.
227. RODINSON (Maxime), *op. cit.* pp. 168, 188, 204, 300 and 310.
228. RODINSON (Maxime), *op. cit.* p. 242.
229. *Ibid*, p. 248.
230. *Ibid*, p. 257.
231. *Ibid*, p. 305.
232. HUSSEIN (Mahmoud), *op. cit.* volume I, p. 473; volume II, pp. 50, 335 and 423.
233. See *Le Coran, op. cit.* p. 560; HICHÂM (Ibn), *op. cit.* pp. 212 and 294; HUSSEIN (Mahmoud), *op. cit.* volume I, p. 405; RODINSON (Maxime), *op. cit.* p. 108.
234. *Ibid*, p. 232.

the richest among us. If you aim at rank, we will make you our leader and will not settle any dispute without your agreement. If you aim at the throne, we will make you our king.[235] Muhammad rejected these proposals.

He made this self-control a divine commandment: "Do not obey...anyone who allows himself to be led by his passions and who is careless in his behavior."[236] With the notable exception of sudden angers and early revelations, Muhammad hardly experienced any psychological crises. He regulated his life with habits[237] and rituals[238]. He made this a divine commandment: "Be constant!"[239]

The last point to note is that Muhammad was absolutely certain that he had the truth. He repeated it over and over again[240]. "This is the absolute truth!"[241] The word *certainty* probably had another meaning in those early days, so that Jesus claimed it in order to declare himself "son of God", and Muhammad the opposite.

Thus, this last one manifested a whole character, a strong propensity to the binary choices, an exceptional obstinacy, a sharp sense of the duty, an obsession of the purity, an obvious authoritarianism, a notable aggressiveness, a certain emotional coldness,

---

235. HUSSEIN (Mahmoud), *op. cit.* volume I, p. 391.
236. *The Koran, op. cit.* p. 359.
237. HUSSEIN (Mahmoud), *op. cit.* volume I, p. 512.
238. *Ibid. in* Volume II, p. 271.
239. *The Koran, op. cit.* p. 587.
240. *Ibid,* pp. 4, 7, 146, 351, 416, 424, 610, 620, 621, 628 and 648; HUSSEIN (Mahmoud), *op. cit.* volume I, pp. 340 and 397; volume II, p. 33.
241. *The Koran, op. cit.* p. 672.

a certain greed for the money, a marked taste for the accounts, a mania of the calculation, a tendency to the intellectualization and the very asserted feeling to hold indisputable truths.

All these symptoms are part of what psychologists call the "obsessive personality", otherwise known as "anal character". As we explained with the case of Jesus[242], these traits originate in an unconscious struggle against opposite infantile tendencies, mainly destructive aggressiveness and the pleasure of messing up. The result is a very organized, meticulous, planning, stubborn character, who likes to purify everything and put it into precise categories, with constraining rules, including his own actions and feelings.

We begin to guess at some elements to explain the so particular destiny of the Muhammad case. His hallucinations in his forties opened a crisis in his relationships with his relatives. His anal character must have contributed to transform this inner voice into laws. This obsessive personality also proved useful in organizing his political dealings and battle plans. His exceptional vindictiveness and stubbornness would finally have given the necessary push to impose such false ideas, but so well presented, to the naturally reluctant crowds. Let us note in passing the resolution of a revealing contradiction: he swung between anger and impassivity, between direct aggression and anal retentiveness. His fundamental hatred was permanently opposed to attempts to control his affect - an

---

242. JOI (Frédéric), *op. cit.* pp. 41-44.

internal struggle that must have been epic. This channelling of his aggression was to make it even more effective in the long run.

We are far from finished with the complex and pathological personality of Muhammad... We wonder how his contemporaries managed it, not without compassion for them.

CHAPTER FOUR

THE QUERULOUS CHARACTER OF MUHAMMAD

The condition to fit two identities under the same skull is to have a large ego.

This is a joke. Once we put aside his alleged relationship to God, we are forced to admit that Muhammad was only talking about himself and his mission[243]. "The people of Medina and the Bedouins around them should not be left behind the Prophet of God, nor should they prefer their own lives to his.[244] This egocentric trait was also apparent in the fact that the examples he chose were always from his own small, very localized life, and never extended to the wider world or to universality[245].

In these conditions, Muhammad believed himself to be at the center of interests, he interpreted every-thing according to himself[246]. "He was the one whom

---

243. See in particular *Le Coran, op. cit.* pp. 230, 381 and 684; HICHÂM (Ibn), *op. cit.* p. 407.
244. *The Koran, op. cit.* p. 244.
245. *Ibid,* p. 674.
246. *Ibid. at* 150 and 230; Rodinson (Maxime), *op. cit.* at 201.

the Supreme Being was concerned with, he whom he had created and whom he would judge without consideration of kinship, family, tribe."[247] When God chooses you personally, it makes you a man. Especially if the opposite had really happened: that Muhammad had chosen to interpret his inner way as that of God who had chosen him...

This excessive self-love, which psychiatrists call "autophilia", was reflected in his affection for his own works, for which he could not find sufficient praise[248]. His inner voice made the jinn say, "Yes, we have heard a wonderful Qur'an!"[249] Elsewhere he spoke of the "glorious Qur'an"[250], or the "wise Qur'an"[251]. He thought that he had made the religion perfect[252], that he had spoken about everything that exists[253], etc.

More than an absence of self-criticism, Muhammad showed a very high opinion of himself[254]. He considered himself good[255], wise[256], intelligent[257], useful[258],

---

247. *Ibid*, p. 126.
248. *The Qur'an, op. cit.* pp. 253, 263, 351, 424, 589, 606, 686, 724 and 750.
249. *Ibid*, p. 721.
250. *Ibid*, p. 643.
251. *Ibid*, p. 540.
252. *Ibid*, p. 125.
253. *Ibid.* at 159 and 256.
254. See in particular *Le Coran, op. cit.* pp. 743-744; HICHÂM (Ibn), *op. cit.* pp. 54, 145 and 156; RODINSON (Maxime), *op. cit.* p. 80.
255. *The Koran, op. cit.* p. 246.
256. *Ibid*, p. 463.
257. *Ibid,* pp. 157, 303 and 585.
258. *Ibid*, p. 268.

overpowered[259], etc. His inner voice itself seemed to be subservient to this oversized ego, with Gabriel stating, "Never, I swear, was any prophet before Muhammad... better than he was in the sight of God."[260] Following a more than ordinary parable, we saw him engage in an astonishing exercise of "self-congratulation", like a sportsman who asks the spectators to watch his great deed again in slow motion: "Did you not see how God proposes a very good word in a parable? It is like an excellent tree with a strong root, a branch in the sky and abundant fruit in every season [...]"[261]

All these features revealed his "strong personality", not easily influenced by others.

We discover another list of remarkable symptoms with the permanent hallucinations that he endured, at least from his forties onwards, and for a good twenty years[262]. He experienced a waking dream state (called "oniroid" by specialists), with visionary experiences, a feeling of strangeness and a "hypermnesia" (overdeveloped memory) that allowed him to repeat whole sections of the Bible. Maxime Rodinson rightly notes: "These hallucinations, these ecstasies also worry the believing psychiatrists of today because, honestly, they are forced to recognize that nothing

---

259. *Ibid,* p. 189.
260. HICHÂM (Ibn), *op. cit.* p. 140.
261. *The Koran, op. cit.* p. 311.
262. *Ibid,* p. 436; HICHÂM (Ibn), *op. cit.* pp. 79, 80, 140-141, 146 and 180; HUSSEIN (Mahmoud), *op. cit.* volume I, pp. 453-460; volume II, pp. 152, 366 and 367; RODINSON (Maxime), *op. cit.* pp. 97, 105 and 108.

formally distinguishes those of the mystics from those of the sick."[263]

Alongside these hallucinations, an astonishing phenomenon appeared: Muhammad was constantly attributing to others what was valid for him - in the language of psychiatrists: projections.

He often attributed his own hatred to others[264]. Let us admire for a moment this superb tirade, comparing its beginning and its end (which we underline): "The Prophet answered: "Ha! these unfortunate Qurayshites! *They are devoured by the demon of war.* What would they lose if they left me alone to fight all the other Arabs? If I am defeated, they will have got what they want. If, on the contrary, God gives me victory, they will enter Islam richer. *I will not stop fighting, I swear,* for the mission that God has entrusted to me, until victory or death."[265]

He very often projected his own situation, including his unmentionable folly, onto the earlier prophets, especially Moses and Noah: "The leaders of his people, who were unbelievers, said, 'We see your folly! We consider you a liar!'"[266]

He blamed God for his own mania to legislate: "He commands them what is proper; he declares lawful for them the excellent foods; he declares unlawful for

---

263. RODINSON (Maxime), *op. cit.* p. 107.
264. See especially *The Koran, op. cit.* pp. 77 and 234.
265. HICHÂM (Ibn), *op. cit.* p. 300.
266. *The Koran, op. cit.* pp. 189 and 632.

them what is detestable [...]"[267] He also projected his greed: "You want the goods of this world."[268]

On many occasions he attributed to others his own stubbornness, "...there are stubborn hypocrites"[269], his habit of inventing divine stories, "they let themselves be led astray in their religion by their own inventions"[270], or of resorting to lies (the "tricks of war" or great religious impostures, such as paradise, etc.)[271]. We propose another superb projection, in which he began with a shameless lie by attributing to Jesus a sentence that we challenge you to find in the Gospels, to end with a firework display (emphasis added): "Jesus, son of Mary, said: 'O son of Israel! I am indeed the Prophet of God sent to you to confirm what was before me in the Torah; to bring you *good news of a Prophet who will come after me, whose name will be 'Ahmad.*" But when he came to them with unquestionable evidence, they said, "This is obvious sorcery!" *Who then is more unjust than one who forges a lie against God* while he is called to Submission?"[272]

Rather than modestly admitting that no one can know for sure whether God exists, he blithely blamed this ignorance on atheists: "They say, 'There is only our present life for us: we live and we die. Only the passing

---

267. *Ibid,* pp. 187, and 203-204.
268. *Ibid,* p. 222.
269. *Ibid,* pp. 241 and 719.
270. HUSSEIN (Mahmud), *op. cit.* volume II, p. 54; *The Koran, op. cit.* pp. 334, 337, 338 and 397.
271. *Ibid,* pp. 355, and 681-682.
272. *Ibid,* p. 692.

of time makes us perish." They have no knowledge of any of this; they are only engaged in conjecture."[273]

He who believed himself to be at the center of the universe, with his privileged place assigned by God, and who imagined himself constantly insulted, dared to say: "They think that every cry is directed against them."[274]

Generally speaking, Muhammad painted his own portrait believing that he was painting that of others, to whom he kindly attributed impatience[275], pride[276], vanity[277], transgression of the law[278], political calculation[279], love of disputes[280], mockery, slander and defamation[281], change of traditions[282], venality[283], etc.[284] We keep one last one for the good mouth. He who lied about paradise, he who produced serial projections, accomplished the following tour de force: "They attribute to God what they hate for themselves. Their tongues speak lies when they say that a good reward

---

273. *Ibid*, p. 620. See also other projections of ignorance, pp. 355 and 750.
274. *Ibid*, p. 696.
275. *Ibid.* at 399.
276. *Ibid*, pp. 423, 696 and 719.
277. *Ibid*, p. 495.
278. *Ibid*, p. 187.
279. *Ibid*, p. 335.
280. *Ibid*, p. 610.
281. *Ibid*, pp. 641 and 710.
282. *Ibid*, p. 455.
283. See Rodinson (Maxime), *op. cit.* p. 116, quotation from the *Koran*, Sura LXXXIX, verses 18-21.
284. Little game: find the projections in *The Koran, op. cit.* pp. 216, 382, 421, 456 and 630.

awaits them.[285] This one alone should have been written in the Qur'an: a projection of projections!

Muhammad also made some "megaprojections" or "mythic projections", that is, projections of structures of the collective unconscious[286], such as the myth of a universal father, namely God. Although numerous, they are only repetitions of inventions of previous prophets[287]. At best, we find only naive descriptions of paradise, so much so that manifest basic desires appear, very relative to its geographical and historical situation[288].

On the basis of these hallucinations and projections, Muhammad had constructed an interpretation of himself. To affirm that he claimed to be a messiah, a prophet, a mystic, etc.[289], is a petition of principle. We must specify this because these words designate for psychiatrists as many pathological symptoms identified among a certain type of seriously ill patients interned in hospitals. The latter claim to have made a brilliant discovery, to be revolutionary or to have understood everything. They believe that they are the exception, that they are the only ones who understand, that they must save the world by generously distributing their ideas or their wealth. They are assured of posthumous glory, of having a destiny, a historical

---

285. *Ibid*, p. 330.
286. See JOI (Frédéric), *op. cit.* pp. 109-147.
287. See especially *The Qur'an, op. cit.* pp. 20, 22, 45, 46, 336, 407, 613, 644 and 646.
288. *Ibid*, p. 669.
289. *Ibid*, p. 686; HICHÂM (Ibn), *op. cit*, pp. 100, 173, 381 and 393.

importance, a mission to accomplish[290]. For such patients, psychiatrists still note the impression of being influenced, with inner dialogues and a tendency to the supernatural. The Qur'an contains a large number of dialogues, which corresponded to several characters in conversation in Muhammad's mind.

While Muhammad acknowledged copying his predecessors, he developed what psychiatrists call a "plagiarism delusion": "The Prophet said, 'The hour of judgment will not have come until thirty impostors appear, each claiming to be a prophet.[291] He developed another delusion well known to their hospital services, which consists in believing himself to be immortal (let us put here in his defense that, in the following scene, Muhammad was suffering from the physical illness that would take him away): "Then the Prophet approached Abû Muwayha and confided to him:

- I was given the keys to the treasures of the earth with the ability to live there forever, and on the other side I was put in Paradise. I was given the choice between eternal treasures on earth and meeting God, and then Paradise.

- I beg you," exclaimed Abû Muwayha, "choose the keys of the treasures of the earth to live there eternally, then Paradise.

---

290. *Le Coran, op. cit.* p. 510; HICHÂM (Ibn), *op. cit.* pp. 100 and 156.
291. *Ibid*, p. 384; *The Qur'an, op. cit*, p. 15.

- No, no," replied the Prophet, "I have chosen the meeting with my God and Paradise."[292]

It was a close call.

We also find in Muhammad ideas of grandeur, but only a few, if we discard those he took from the Bible. He imagined that the Qur'an could break a mountain[293] or that its message would be heard from one end of the earth to the other[294].

Apart from the very beautiful "delusion of filiation", which deserves to be given a whole chapter, we discover a last delusion very often manifested by Muhammad. He was extremely jealous. He was certainly possessive of his wives, which could explain in part his delusion of the attire to be hidden[295]: "O you, the wives of the Prophet ! Whoever of you is guilty of a manifest turpitude, she shall receive twice the punishment. This is easy for God. [Stay in your houses, do not show yourselves in your finery as women did in the time of ancient ignorance."[296]

He was still jealous of the believers, whose love, attention and intentions he wanted to monopolize, just as Jesus did[297]: "Do not let your wealth and your children distract you from the remembrance of God!"[298]

---

292. HICHÂM (Ibn), *op. cit.* pp. 402-403.

293. *The Koran, op. cit.* p. 686.

294. HUSSEIN (Mahmoud), *op. cit.* volume II, p. 261.

295. On the issue of women's veiling, see *The Qur'an, op. cit.* pp. 434, 439, 522 and 523.

296. *The Koran, op. cit.* p. 518.

297. JOI (Frédéric), *op. cit.* pp. 74-75.

298. *The Qur'an, op. cit.* p. 696. See also pp. 243 and 699.

This relationship with the beautiful sex is all the more surprising since "the women whom the Prophet married were thirteen"[299]. He consummated eleven of his marriages[300]. He refrained from enjoying one of them as soon as he discovered skin spots that betrayed the leprosy of his newly wed wife[301]. He never resisted beautiful women, especially among the captives of his conquests[302]. He had an extraordinary sexual appetite[303], so much so that he was insulted by his lucid contemporaries, the Banû Quraydha: "This man devotes his energy to women and the pleasure of the flesh. If he were a true prophet, as he claims, prophecy would occupy him more than women![304] This is not the case with Aisha who will deny them[305]: "[Muhammad] went to the house of Abû Bakr and on the way saw 'Â'isha playing with some friends on a swing."[306] "She was, it is true, only six years old. That was too little, even for Arabs." [307]

"He liked it. [It was then objected to him:]

- But we have daughters older than her.

---

299. HICHÂM (Ibn), *op. cit.* p. 399. See pp. 399-401 for details of these marriages.
300. *Ibid*, p. 401.
301. *Ibid.*
302. *Ibid*, pp. 291 and 316; HUSSEIN (Mahmoud), *op. cit.* volume II, p. 402; RODINSON (Maxime), *op. cit.* pp. 230 and 247.
303. See in particular *Le Coran, op. cit.* pp. 667 and 669; HUSSEIN (Mahmoud), *op. cit.* volume II, pp. 207 and 371-372; Rodinson (Maxime), *op. cit.* pp. 75, 291 and 316.
304. HUSSEIN (Mahmoud), *op. cit.* volume II, p. 348.
305. *Ibid*, vol. I, pp. 461-463, vol. II, p. 34; RODINSON (Maxime), *op. cit*, pp. 165, 182, 232 and 234.
306. *Ibid. in* Volume I, p. 462.
307. *Ibid*, p. 165.

- It is 'Â'isha that I want. [...]

- Can 'isha be suitable for the Messenger of God, even though she is his brother's daughter? [...]

- I am his brother and he is my brother and I can marry his daughter."[308]

She said: "The Messenger of God married me when I was six years old and the wedding was celebrated when I was nine.[309] Maxime Rodinson adds: "The ceremony was reduced to its simplest expression. The little girl was left with her toys and dolls and Mohammad sometimes played with her.[310]

The term used in psychiatry for this frantic quest for women is *don juanism*, even if Muhammad did not only use his charm to lead them to his bed[311]. We could speak of a manifest "lack of love", probably due to an orphaned and disinherited childhood. This obsessive motive was indirectly inscribed in the great number of laws that he promulgated on sexuality in general[312] and women in particular[313].

This passion for the beautiful sex was accompanied by an exceptional energy that he spent in a

---

308. HUSSEIN (Mahmoud), *op. cit.* volume I, p. 462.
309. Quoted by RODINSON (Maxime), *op. cit.* p. 182.
310. *Ibid.*
311. See HICHÂM (Ibn), *op. cit.* p. 401, quotation from the Koran; RODINSON (Maxime), *op. cit.* p. 289.
312. See in particular *Le Coran, op. cit.* pp. 37, 42, 96, 97, 344, 419, 434, 518, 519, 521 and 717; HICHÂM (Ibn), *op. cit.* p. 135; HUSSEIN (Mahmoud), *op. cit.* volume II, pp. 80, 81, 177 and 389.
313. See especially *The Qur'an, op. cit.* pp. 43, 44, 434, 436, 523, 678, 679, 689, 690, 700 and 705.

great number of projects[314]. Psychiatrists speak of "hypersthenia".

Muhammad's impulsiveness was reflected in his relationship to knowledge. He displayed a passionate idealism, with great vigor in the defense of his ideas. Psychiatrists speak of "logorrhea" or "ideorrhea," which means "flow of ideas. As we have seen, he wanted to be right all the time, was obsessed with the truth, and believed that he alone possessed it: "[God] knows the mystery perfectly; but he shows no one the secret of his mystery, except to him whom he accepts as a prophet."[315]

Eager for meaning, Muhammad nourished a desire for universal knowledge. He denied chance and coincidences, with his famous "fatalism"[316]. He interpreted everything, everything had to have a meaning, everything was a "sign"[317]. He repeated over and over again that "[God] exposes the Signs for the people who know"[318].

He forged his knowledge alone, by simple hearsay and personal reconstruction. With the exception of a mystical period when he imitated other ascetics[319], he had invented his "craft", demonstrating self-didacticism. His initial ideas proved to be false, such as the assertion that God spoke to him through Gabriel, that he was a prophet, that Heaven and Hell exist, etc.

---

314. See in particular HICHÂM (Ibn), *op. cit.,* pp. 180 and 372.
315. *The Koran, op. cit.* p. 723.
316. *Ibid,* p. 484.
317. *Ibid,* p. 299.
318. *Ibid,* p. 247.
319. See RODINSON (Maxime), *op. cit.* pp. 95 ff.

These are what psychiatrists call "delusions", etymologically ideas that come out of the groove. On these basic ideas he built a vast "system" that was intended to be coherent, with only apparent logic and argumentative dialectics to defend it. He was constantly trying to account for everything on the basis of his false ideas. As Maxime Rodinson says: "This ideology forms a system."[320]

With great bad faith, Muhammad explained why he won this battle (God was comforting him of course), but also, in a convoluted way, why he lost that one: "If you have received a wound, these people have received a wound. We make the days (good and bad) alternate among people so that Allah may know the faithful and choose witnesses from among you (and Allah does not love the unjust), to make those who believe shine and cast the disbelievers into the shadows."[321]

He was constantly justifying himself[322]. He "legitimized" his plundering[323], his very personal use of alms[324], the invasion of a Jewish city[325], the destruction[326], the murder[327], etc.

He did not suffer contradiction. He was enraged that the ungodly did not attribute their happiness to

---

320. *Ibid*, p. 271.
321. *Ibid*, p. 217, from the *Qur'an*, Sura III, verses 160-162.
322. See in particular *Le Coran, op. cit.* pp. 315, 519 and 631; HUSSEIN (Mahmoud), *op. cit.* volume II, pp. 110 and 205; Rodinson (Maxime), *op. cit.* p. 220.
323. *The Koran, op. cit.* p. 171.
324. *Ibid*, p. 233.
325. *Ibid*, p. 205.
326. *The Koran, op. cit.* p. 342.
327. HICHÂM (Ibn), *op. cit.* p. 169.

God[328], that they did not believe in one of his revelations[329], that they did not obey when he ordered Abû Bakr to preside over a public prayer[330], etc. When his ignorance of the Old Testament was confronted with the Jews, "the mockery and criticism of their intellectuals irritated him and we saw how sensitive he was to such attacks"[331].

However, if no one came to tickle him on his delirium, his partial madness left intact the other mental activities. He showed an intelligence and knowledge superior to the average of the people of the time[332], which remains very relative. In this respect, he was able to impress a simple servant, a certain 'Addâs: "I do not know anyone on this earth who is better than him. He taught me what only a prophet can know."[333]

Maxime Rodinson sums up perfectly this typical contrast between the rationality and the delusions of Muhammad: "He reasons clearly, logically, with lucidity. And yet, behind all this facade, there is a nervous, passionate, anxious, feverish temperament, full of impatient and ardent aspirations for the impossible. This went as far as nervous crises of a completely pathological nature."[334]

---

328. *The Koran, op. cit.* p. 165.
329. *Ibid,* p. 166.
330. HICHÂM (Ibn), *op. cit.* p. 406.
331. RODINSON (Maxime), *op. cit.* p. 202.
332. HICHÂM (Ibn), *op. cit,* pp. 153 and 388; RODINSON (Maxime), *op. cit,* p. 73
333. HUSSEIN (Mahmoud), *op. cit.* volume I, p. 475.
334. RODINSON (Maxime), *op. cit.* p. 77.

With such traits, he was very "convincing"[335]... let's be clear: without resorting to force. He used beautiful (poetic) words[336], showed an undeniable charisma[337], and among his zealots were people who had initially hated him[338].

Insofar as the ideas that he managed to impose were false, we must see in this a simple mechanism well known to psychiatrists, called "delusion with two". One of the two protagonists is at the origin of the delirium, and has an ascendancy over the second, who ends up adhering to the false idea, to develop it in turn in a pathological way. Such a psychological contagion appeared clearly in at least two cases, on the one hand between Muhammad and Ali, his young - not to say "naive" - cousin (converted at the age of ten![339]), and on the other hand between Muhammad and his faithful Abû Bakr. The latter very quickly acted as a relay for the ideas of his master: "Abû Bakr preached [...] Islam to visitors in whom he had confidence. Many of the Prophet's companions came to know Islam through Abû Bakr."[340]

Muhammad occasionally exhibited an incredible lucidity about himself. Most of the time he did not

---

335. See in particular HICHÂM (Ibn), *op. cit.* pp. 63, 87, 90, 92, 114, 121, 138 and 172; HUSSEIN (Mahmud), *op. cit.* volume I, pp. 327, 358, 384 and 448; volume II, p. 82.

336. See in particular HICHÂM (Ibn), *op. cit.* pp. 99 and 133; HUSSEIN (Mahmud), *op. cit.* volume I, pp. 387, 393 and 466.

337. See in particular HICHÂM (Ibn), *op. cit.* p. 303; HUSSEIN (Mahmud), *op. cit.* volume I, p. 354; volume II, p. 394.

338. *Ibid. in* Volume II, p. 83.

339. HICHÂM (Ibn), *op. cit.* p. 86.

340. *Ibid,* p. 88.

express it directly, but made the characters in his biblical stories who rejected the old prophets say: "We see in you only a mortal like ourselves. We see you, at first sight, followed only by the most contemptible among us. We do not see in you any superiority over us. On the contrary, we think you are liars."[341], "This is more like a heap of dreams that he has invented himself; he is a poet!"[342], "These are the tales of the ancients!"[343] Sometimes Muhammad betrayed himself in a way by denying the characterization that fit him like a glove: "This is not an imagined tale [...]"[344] Sometimes again, he directly acknowledged: "God has sent down the most beautiful of tales: a Book whose parts resemble and repeat each other."[345] We confirm.

This egocentrism and enthusiastic prophetism, based on his own hallucinatory knowledge, encouraged by a solid aggressiveness and a very organized obstinacy, could not fail to lead to conflicting relations with his contemporaries, in a "persecutory" mode.

"O you who believe! Make friends only among yourselves; others will not fail to harm you; they want your loss; hatred is manifested in their mouths, but what is hidden in their hearts is worse. [You love them, and they do not love you..."[346] Many passages of this type

---

341. *The Koran, op. cit.* p. 267.
342. *The Koran, op. cit.* p. 396.
343. *Ibid,* p. 746.
344. *Ibid,* p. 298.
345. *Ibid,* p. 569.
346. *Ibid,* pp. 77-78.

show a feeling of persecution[347]. Muhammad liked to repeat the stories of earlier prophets who were bullied by their peoples[348]. This generalized distrust is found throughout[349]. He was suspicious of false obedience[350] or of other prophets[351]. Gabriel himself is said to have enjoined suspicion on him, allegedly allowing him to escape an assassination attempt, "Do not sleep tonight in the place where you usually sleep."[352] This mindset had spread among all his followers: "During the last ten years they had spent in Makkah, the Messenger of God and his companions had lived on their guard. And when God had ordered them to leave Makkah for Madinah, they had settled there on their guard. By day and by night they had their weapons at hand."[353]

Muhammad believed that he was always being watched, if only by God: "There is no meeting of three where he is not the fourth, nor of five where he is not the sixth. Whether they are fewer or more in number, he is with them wherever they are, and on the Day of Judgment he will make known to them what they have done. - Verily, God knows everything"[354]

347. See in particular HICHÂM (Ibn), *op. cit.* pp. 82 and 200; HUSSEIN (Mahmud), *op. cit.* volume II, p. 196.
348. RODINSON (Maxime), *op. cit.* p. 151.
349. HICHÂM (Ibn), *op. cit.* p. 245; HUSSEIN (Mahmoud), *op. cit.* volume I, p. 411; volume II, pp. 281 and 346; RODINSON (Maxime), *op. cit.* p. 168.
350. *The Koran, op. cit.* p. 235.
351. *Ibid*, p. 640.
352. HICHÂM (Ibn), *op. cit.* p. 172.
353. HUSSEIN (Mahmoud), *op. cit.* volume II, p. 89.
354. *The Koran, op. cit.* p. 679.

He had the constant feeling that conspiracies were being hatched behind his back, that slander was being spread without his knowledge or that spies were operating in the shadows[355]. Fortunately for him, Allah was there to "... warn him... that such plots were afoot..."[356]

In such patients, psychiatrists note a time lag between the onset of the delusion and its fixation in a pseudo-rational system. It is in this in-between period that therapists must intervene, when possible. Maxime Rodinson describes very well this slow passage between the first revelations and their setting in a system. Let's quote some excerpts: "One day, unexpectedly, a voice was heard. It was undoubtedly the first time that the sensation of something extraordinary was so precise, without which one would not explain the emotion of the pious Mekkois. The Voice said three Arabic words that were to shock the world: "You are the Envoy of God!" [...] How did this revelation and the following ones come about, in what chronological order? One cannot know it exactly. Without doubt their form became progressively more precise. After the sensations of supernatural presence, the vague visions, the hearing of simple sentences, came the long series of well-ordered words, offering a clear meaning, a message. [...] Later, when Mohammad had become accustomed to the idea of his exceptional destiny,

---

355. *Ibid,* pp. 151, 395, 471 and 680.
356. RODINSON (Maxime), *op. cit.* p. 225.

there came the terror of having been mistaken [...]"[357] Before being certain of his fact, Mohammad experienced long residual doubts[358].

He suffered greatly from mockery, which he constantly complained about[359]. "When the disbelievers see you, they only mock you, "Is this the one who vilifies your gods?" They do not believe in the Reminder of the Merciful."[360] Let us admit that he was particularly touchy[361]. It was even because he was offended by Jews that Muhammad changed the direction of prayer, or *qibla*. At the beginning of Islam, Muslims were supposed to face Jerusalem, but then: "... it came to the ears of the Messenger of God that the Jews said, 'By God, Muhammad and his companions did not know in which direction to pray, until we offered them our *qibla*. The Messenger of God hated that anyone would say this. He looked up to the sky and the Most High revealed to him, "We often see your face turned to the sky. So we will give you a *qibla that is* pleasing to you. Turn your face in the direction of the Sacred Mosque.[362]

---

357. *The Koran, op. cit.* p. 97.
358. See in particular HICHÂM (Ibn), *op. cit.* p. 105; RODINSON (Maxime), *op. cit.* p. 99.
359. See especially *The Qur'an, op. cit.* pp. 39, 137, 150, 232, 305, 316, 363, 450, 505 and 618.
360. *Ibid.* at 399.
361. *Ibid*, pp. 248, 250, 505 and 748; HICHÂM (Ibn), *op. cit*, pp. 84 and 366; HUSSEIN (Mahmud), *op. cit*, vol. II, pp. 83 and 407; RODINSON (Maxime), *op. cit*, pp. 202 and 208.
362. HUSSEIN (Mahmoud), *op. cit.* volume II, p. 109.

As a result of this mistrust, Muhammad became very observant of the people around him[363]. He even boasted: "I know what you hide and what you disclose.[364] He used this trait to manipulate men: "Mohammad, moreover, is endowed to the highest degree with the essential virtue of the *sayyid*, the Arab leader, the *hilm*, a patient and tenacious skill in handling men through knowledge of their interests and their passions. He knows how to intelligently, without constraint and without outbursts, obtain in the end the acquiescence of his followers to the decisions he has taken."[365]

When his contemporaries rejected his ravings, Muhammad felt misunderstood[366]. He had a strong sense of injustice, which manifested itself in his repeated reminders: "Be fair! God loves those who are fair!"[367] He constantly feared being betrayed or deceived[368] : "When the hypocrites come to you, they say, "We testify that you are the Prophet of God!" [They have taken their oaths as a safeguard and have strayed from the path of God. What they have done is detestable."[369]

Paradoxically, Muhammad relieved himself of the weight of laws, both moral and clan-based, according

---

363. See in particular *Le Coran, op. cit.* pp. 235, 330, 421, 427, 644 and 703; HUSSEIN (Mahmoud), *op. cit.* volume I, p. 344.

364. *The Koran, op. cit.* p. 688.

365. RODINSON (Maxime), *op. cit.* p. 255.

366. See especially *The Koran, op. cit.* pp. 15 and 614.

367. *Le Coran, op. cit.* p. 640. See also pp. 116, 127 and 276; Rodinson (Maxime), *op. cit.* p. 334.

368. See especially *The Qur'an, op. cit.* pp. 216, 236, 513 and 515.

369. *The Koran, op. cit.* p. 695.

to the needs of the moment, without necessarily realizing it. In general, after a murder, a raid, a genocide, his conscience was lightened by the intimate conviction that God had wanted it. He did the same with lies[370], when his own interest was at stake. To deceive an enemy sheikh, he delegated a man to get rid of him by treachery. The latter "was allowed to say anything, to curse the Prophet if necessary, to gain the confidence of the sheikh [...]"[371] He was also capable of remarkable bad faith: "I have none of the intentions you attribute to me. In my mission to you, I seek neither money, nor honor, nor power."[372] Even worse, he who suddenly insulted the Quraysh after his revelations, dared to say (emphasis added): "Are you not fighting people who violated their oaths and sought to expel the Prophet? It was *they who first attacked you.*"[373]

An amusing personality trait will conclude this edifying catalog with a bang: incurability. Despite the years, the adversaries, the old age, Muhammad never let his guard down, to develop all these beautiful symptoms with an admirable assiduity.

To sum up, we put forward the hypothesis of an extremely vindictive Muhammad, with a solidly organized character, a particularly swollen ego, hallucinations and other projections galore, a manifest prophetic delirium, a passionate idealism based on the certainty of all knowledge, from which stemmed a

---

370. *Ibid*, pp. 268, 271 and 502; HICHÂM (Ibn), *op. cit*, pp. 249 and 268; HUSSEIN (Mahmud), *op. cit*, vol. II, pp. 205 and 227.
371. RODINSON (Maxime), *op. cit.* p. 222.
372. HICHÂM (Ibn), *op. cit.* p. 100.
373. *The Koran, op. cit.* p. 225.

relationship tinged with persecution with his contemporaries, who were necessarily sceptical.

These traits betray a paranoia. Let us recall the operating principle of this serious pathology[374].

The self of the subject rejects the reality commonly admitted by all in the name of its unconscious impulses, and rebuilds its own universe by hallucinations and projections of its interiority. He begins by withdrawing his interest from the world, to then reinvest it in his own way, by arranging it according to his desires. Muhammad did have an ascetic period, withdrawing into a cave. Already in his childhood, he had to flee from the harsh reality, to take refuge in an imaginary world.

In this movement of return on oneself of the impulse, the subject rejects reality, the society, the prohibitions, and all that does not satisfy directly its self. He gets rid of the external limits and the negative opinions on himself. He loves himself in an exclusive way, by refusing the self-criticisms. His moral conscience starts to function in reverse mode: such subjects congratulate themselves, give themselves as a model to follow, and assert laws to others. An immense amount of energy is released in this way. Muhammad did not bother with internal barriers to impose his views.

By forging a universe of his own, hallucinated, the paranoid creates false ideas, "delusions". There are many varieties, of which persecution is only one example. Muhammad seems to have developed at

---

374. JOI (Frédéric), *op. cit.* pp. 75-81.

least delusions of jealousy, immortality, plagiarism, prophetism, grandeur, persecution, and filiation.

The origin of these delusions lies in projection. Persecution consists in attributing one's own hatred to others, and believing oneself to be hated by them. The delusion of immortality consists in projecting the atemporality proper to the unconscious. The delusion of plagiarism is explained by the fact of imputing to others the same unconscious mechanisms as one's own, at the origin of the alleged prophecy. The subject then fears that others will act like him. The delusion of interpretation consists in relating everything to oneself, in believing oneself to be at the center of the universe, because of a disproportionate ego, for the benefit of which the subject reconstructs the world. The delusion of grandeur (or megalomania) also results from this ego, which takes up all the space in the subject's psyche. The prophetic delusion is born of the projection onto reality of the return of the love drive onto oneself, with an inverted functioning of the moral conscience. Just as the latter encourages the self of the subject, a supreme father would exist in the sky who chose him, who loves him, who supports him, and who gives him laws to be imposed on all.

According to Freud, jealousy arises from a projection of his own unconscious homosexual desires onto his wife. The jealous person thinks that it is she who desires other men, and not himself. Don Juanism shares the same psychological spring. It lies in the internal struggle against strong homosexual tendencies by constantly reassuring oneself of one's own heterosexuality, with ever more proof: "Yes, it is indeed women I desire", Muhammad could say to himself at each new wedding.

The particularity of the paranoid consists in defending these delusions, against all odds, within the framework of a vast and apparently logical systematization. This is the contribution of the anal character, where the subject delights in organizing everything, legislating, taking stock, etc. In the case of Muhammad, the resulting system became particularly visible, and materialized in this book which he called "Koran".

We now have enough evidence to propose some hypotheses. Muhammad was distinguished in that his main misconception, that he was called by God, originated in a dissociative disorder. The ideas imposed by his second identity, which we can call with him "Gabriel", were then taken up and systematized by his first, paranoid identity.

Muhammad, before he heard this voice, had a strong personality. If he was initially shaken, the next twenty years undoubtedly saw his slow recovery of his cracked interiority. Insensibly, he regained control of his second identity, to put it at the service of his own designs. At the beginning, he had to be satisfied to obey it, to put himself "modestly" to its service, by systematizing it. Then, his first identity, so energetic and structured, took over. In the end, Gabriel appeared only as a tool in the service of Muhammad's goals. We assume that this second identity became nothing more than a blob reintegrated into the first. Muhammad thus proceeded to a kind of reverse self-medication: instead of submitting his false ideas to reality by reintegrating his second identity into society, he imposed them by force on others, through a first identity which was itself very sick. The dissociative disorder was integrated into the paranoia, and even instrumentalized.

To refine this diagnosis, let us call upon Kretschmer, a psychiatrist who distinguishes three types of paranoia[375] : the first type is the "combat" type, called "querulous" (which implies the claim). It is the classic paranoia, with conflictual engagement of the subject in the social fabric, which tries to impose its delusional ideas. The second type is content with desiring a better world, reconstructed, without committing itself body and soul to its realization. It is characterized by a passionate idealism, without concrete combat. It is a paranoia of wish, of desire, idealistic. The third type is related to a delusion of relationship, which Kretschmer calls "sensitive paranoia". The patient develops a depressive, emotional, shy, modest personality, with guilt, debates of conscience and feelings of inferiority. As for the causes of these variants, the person who discovered them specifies: "The experience that revolts produces a combat paranoid, the experience that is retained, a sensory paranoid, and an experience fed by the imagination, a desire paranoid. [...] First of all, we have become acquainted with three groups of characterogenic delusional evolution which

---

375. *See KRETSCHMER (Ernst)*, Paranoia and sensitivity. Contribution to the problem of the paranoia and to the psychiatric theory of the character, *Brionne, Montfort, 1963.*

tend to a chronic systematization and which, according to the old clinical terminology, can be defined as paranoid: expansive or combat paranoid, sensory or consciousness paranoid and desire paranoid."[376] The reader will undoubtedly have recognized Muhammad in the fight. This one would then appear to us in all his complexity, allying querulous paranoia for his first identity, and dissociative disorder with his second.

This would be our hypothesis: Muhammad was a "dissociative paranoid". A particularly rare case. A performance.

Before tackling the thankless task of understanding how a starving orphan with such a severe psychological handicap was able to generate such an outpouring of support for his ideas, we must explore two more aspects of his complex personality.

---

376. KRETSCHMER (Ernst), *op. cit.* p. 258.

CHAPTER FIVE
THE COMPLEX PARENTAGE OF MUHAMMAD

Throughout his life, Muhammad seemed to develop a particular care to cultivate problematic relationships with filiation, patterns of identification and common laws to be respected.

As an adult, he seemed to compensate somewhat for his lack of parents by inventing a prestigious ancestry: "Since I was in the marrow of Adam, the nations, in all generations, have not ceased to want to attribute my birth to themselves. In fact, I am descended from the two best lines of the Arabs: Hashim and Zuhra.[377] He also spoke of his "father Abraham"[378], his "friend and brother Moses"[379] and his "brother Jesus"[380]. He liked to compare himself to all the prophets (Moses, Abraham[381], Noah, Houd, Çâlih, Loth, Chu'aïb), especially regarding the disbelief that their message began

---

377. HICHÂM (Ibn), *op. cit.* p. 42.
378. HUSSEIN (Mahmoud), *op. cit.* volume II, p. 85.
379. *Ibid. in* Volume II, p. 49.
380. *Ibid. in* Volume II, p. 85.
381. See in particular *Le Coran, op. cit.* p. 401.

to encounter[382]. When he spoke of them, "at every moment there were traits [glimpsed] or [suspected] that [applied] to Mohammad and his situation"[383]. In these Qur'anic narratives, taken from his inner revelations, "different interlocutors speak to each other"[384]. He kept saying "we" when referring to the actions attributed to God[385], and kept praising his supposed exploits[386]. Surprisingly, he forbade adoption[387].

Symmetrically, his own paternity proved to be problematic: "One of the things he was most sensitive to, strange as it may seem to us, was to be deprived of male heirs. This was a disgrace among the Arabs, as it was among the Semites in general, and the men who suffered from it were called *abtar, which* roughly means "mutilated, amputated".[388] Maxime Rodinson also speaks of the "uneasiness of a man ridiculed for his sterility in males [...]"[389] He partly made up for this other lack by adopting his young cousin 'Alî and a slave offered by his wife, a certain Zayd[390]. Very curiously, in his revelations, he stubbornly denied a particular point of biblical tradition, which saw Jesus as the "son" of God[391] - as if he could not bear that one of his peers had a father and not him.

---

382. *Ibid*, Sura XXVI, pp. 450-461.
383. RODINSON (Maxime), *op. cit.* p. 153.
384. *Ibid*, p. 162.
385. See in particular *Le Coran, op. cit.* p. 479.
386. *Ibid*, pp. 502 and 511.
387. HUSSEIN (Mahmoud), *op. cit.* volume II, pp. 371-373.
388. RODINSON (Maxime), *op. cit.* p. 78. See also pp. 75 and 80.
389. RODINSON (Maxime), *op. cit.* p. 80.
390. *Ibid*, pp. 75-76.
391. See especially *The Koran, op. cit.* pp. 128, 166, 355 and 398.

He made it clear that he was not the "father of believers"[392], with a bad faith that was apparent when he elevated his wives to the rank of "mothers of believers"[393]. In any case, he adopted a very infantilizing attitude towards his "subjects"[394]. He even ordered them to prefer him to their own parents: "We have recommended to man to be good to his father and mother; but if they force you to associate with me that of which you have no knowledge, do not obey them."[395]

Correlating with these uncertainties about his identity and filial status, Muhammad seemed to have a very ambiguous relationship with the law.

On the one hand, he confessed that he did not invent anything[396] and that he took the accounts from the Bible[397], which is confirmed by historians[398]. He said: "Yes, the Qur'an is a revelation from the Lord of the Worlds; the faithful Spirit has descended with it on your heart so that you may be among the warners - it is a revelation in clear Arabic. This was already in the Books of the ancients. Is it not a Sign for them that the teachers of the sons of Israel recognize it?[399] He repeated biblical laws, such as Christian forgiveness[400],

---

392. *Ibid*, p. 520; HUSSEIN (Mahmoud), *op. cit.* volume II, p. 373.
393. *The Koran, op. cit.* p. 514.
394. *Ibid*, p. 606.
395. *Ibid*, p. 488.
396. *Ibid*, pp. 623 and 627; HICHÂM (Ibn), *op. cit*, p. 407.
397. *The Qur'an, op. cit.* pp. 282, 297, 393, 555 and 649.
398. RODINSON (Maxime), *op. cit.* pp. 109, 190-191.
399. *The Qur'an, op. cit.* p. 461. See also p. 60.
400. *Ibid*, pp. 9, 59, 90, 206, 577 and 602.

the duty to help the poor[401], the condemnation of greed[402] or Jewish retaliation[403]. The first oath of al-'Aqaba taken by twelve Ansârs to Muhammad confirmed this conformity: "They swore not to associate any god with God, not to steal, not to commit adultery, not to kill their children, not to perjure themselves, not to disobey the Prophet by following the right path."[404] Muhammad was still borrowing the system of the Bible, with Genesis[405], Eden with its apple[406], the Resurrection[407], paradise, the conception of good[408], the notion of "good news"[409], etc.

On the other hand, Muhammad changed the biblical laws, for different reasons. "Our Prophet has come to you. He explains to you a great part of the Book, which you were hiding. He abrogates much of it."[410]

First, he cut through contradictions in the Bible (especially between the Old and New Testaments): "You cannot be Muslims and claim that God has a son, nor can you worship the cross or eat pork."[411] Likewise, he again allowed the divorce forbidden by Jesus[412].

---

401. *Ibid*, p. 647; HUSSEIN (Mahmoud), *op. cit.* volume II, pp. 83 and 108.
402. See in particular *Le Coran, op. cit.* p. 99.
403. *Ibid*, p. 602.
404. HUSSEIN (Mahmoud), *op. cit.* volume I, p. 497.
405. See especially *The Qur'an, op. cit.* pp. 187, 447 and 500.
406. *Ibid*, p. 181.
407. *Ibid*, p. 325.
408. *Ibid*, p. 602.
409. *Ibid*, p. 463.
410. *Ibid*, p. 128.
411. RODINSON (Maxime), *op. cit.* p. 186.
412. See in particular *Le Coran, op. cit.* p. 700; HUSSEIN (Mahmoud), *op. cit.* volume II, p. 212.

Then he could change these laws because of his lack of knowledge of the Bible. The Jewish intellectuals of Medina could not bring themselves to "... enshrine what seemed to them to be the incoherent ravings of an ignorant man, it was difficult not to point out the distortions of the Old Testament narratives in the Qur'an, the anachronisms and errors with which the Qur'an was filled."[413] To counter Jewish criticism, Muhammad claimed to "restore the purity" of their own religion[414].

He could still implicitly modify the biblical laws by adaptation to Arab customs.

Finally, and most importantly, Muhammad changed the laws of the Bible according to particular circumstances and his personal interest. We have already seen that he changed the direction of prayer (*qibla*) because he was personally offended by the Jews[415]. He changed the dates of Jewish fasting, no longer followed their clothing and hair styles following their criticism[416]. For similar reasons, he moved the day of the interruption of trade to Friday[417]. In the interest of a battle, he was willing to remove the guilt from the killing "It was not you who killed them, but God killed them"[418]; to allow himself to fight against the

---

413. RODINSON (Maxime), *op. cit.* p. 192. See also pp. 86, 152 and 218.
414. See in particular HUSSEIN (Mahmoud), *op. cit.* volume II, p. 66.
415. *Ibid*, p. 109.
416. See in particular RODINSON (Maxime), *op. cit.* pp. 202-203.
417. See in particular *Le Coran, op. cit.* p. 694.
418. *Ibid*, p. 214.

Meccan polytheists during the holy months[419], with of course a "good reason" sent down from heaven: "They ask you about fighting in the holy month. Say, "Fighting in this month is a grave sin, but to turn men away from the way of God, to be ungodly to Him and the Sacred Mosque, to drive out its inhabitants, all this is more grave before God."[420] Similarly, we have seen that Muhammad allowed lying to be used as a means of treacherous killing[421]. When he ran out of water, he allowed ablutions with sand[422].

He reached new heights when women were involved. He decreed personal laws on his own wives[423], allowed himself to "take" the women he wanted[424] or to satisfy his sexual needs whenever he pleased, with an image of rare lightness, which women will appreciate: "Your wives are for you a field to plow, go to plow as you please."[425] God, in His infinite mercy, dedicated to him yet another little personalized sweetness: "O you, the Prophet! We have declared the captives lawful for you... as well as any believing woman who has given herself to the Prophet."[426] God

---

419. See in particular RODINSON (Maxime), *op. cit.* p. 195; HUSSEIN (Mahmoud), *op. cit.* volume II, pp. 99, 106 and 107.
420. *The Koran, op. cit.* p. 41.
421. See in particular HUSSEIN (Mahmoud), *op. cit.* volume II, p. 203.
422. *Ibid*, p. 100; *The Qur'an, op. cit*, p. 100.
423. *Ibid*, p. 518.
424. See in particular HUSSEIN (Mahmoud), *op. cit.* volume II, p. 207; *The Koran, op. cit.* pp. 521-522.
425. HUSSEIN (Mahmoud), *op. cit.* volume II, p. 81; *The Koran, op. cit.* p. 43.
426. HICHÂM (Ibn), *op. cit.* p. 401; *The Qur'an, op. cit.* p. 521.

also demanded special respect from Muslims for the wives of a certain Muhammad[427]. Finally, in the delicate matter of the young Aisha being suspected of infidelity, God arranged the matter by requiring no less than four witnesses of adultery[428], which is not found under a horse's hoof. He added the prohibition of slandering honest women[429].

Muhammad did not limit his own insubordination to the Bible. He also copiously misappropriated Arab customs and mores. We can describe these as follows: "The essential thing was not to touch the ancestral rituals, not to abandon the deities worshipped by the ancestors and, finally, to keep the moral values that had made the Arabs great: the code of honor, generosity, hospitality, fidelity to one's word, bravery in battle, etc. One word expresses all these qualities: *murû'a*, the quality of the accomplished man (a bit like the *virtus* of the Romans)."[430] "In reality, the members of these scattered, wandering, famished, terribly anarchic tribes sought to conform to a moral ideal of their own, in the formation of which religion played no part. The model man was endowed to the highest degree with the quality that was called *morouwa*, that is to say etymologically "virility". It included courage, endurance, loyalty to his group and to his social obligations [...]"[431] "[...] in the framework of traditional Arab

---

427. See in particular RODINSON (Maxime), *op. cit.* p. 232.
428. See in particular RODINSON (Maxime), *op. cit.* p. 237; HUSSEIN (Mahmoud), *op. cit.* volume II, pp. 389 and 396.
429. *The Koran, op. cit.* p. 432.
430. HICHÂM (Ibn), *op. cit.* p. 34.
431. RODINSON (Maxime), *op. cit.* p. 38.

social life, inherited from the laws of the desert, it was impossible to escape the infernal cycle of vendettas and counter-vendettas. A fight over a trivial matter between two individuals belonging to different clans could lead, through the interplay of group solidarity and the (ever-changing) alliances of the clans among themselves, to a general war, disastrous for all."[432] "One admired in the Arabs, arrogant and carefree men, not afraid of anything, ready to sacrifice for nothing, for the satisfaction of a beautiful gesture, their lives and their possessions, without thinking about the consequences. What did the contingencies matter, such as the ruin and misery of their family! It was beautiful to give in to one passion after another, to run to death to avenge the smallest insult, to openly despise those disgraced by nature or society [...]"[433]

Again, Muhammad modified these implicit laws for different reasons.

First, he imposed the biblical laws. "The voice from on high recommended only general moral virtues: charity, piety towards God, relative reserve in sexual life, honesty, etc. [Mohammad opposed the presence of God. Yes, God was there and that changed everything. God existed and cared for men, even the humblest ones, He did not want these asocial incursions, disdainful of the interests of tranquility, of the very lives of others. The believer, above all, should take life seriously, think of it in terms of others, of the Good, of the demands of God. [Nothing was more

---

432. *Ibid,* p. 172.
433. *Ibid,* p. 158.

stigmatized than mockery or negligence. Courage and generosity had to be reasonable. One had exalted those who were not afraid of anything. But one had to be afraid. Yes, however shocking it might seem to people brought up in this way, one had to be afraid of God. It was necessary to leave vengeance as much as possible to God, who would not fail to exercise it in the Other World with precautions often disdained by men."[434] Among other changes in Arab morality due to the laws derived from the Bible, we can mention the rejection of infanticide[435], the refusal of the pagan worship of sacred trees in the name of Moses[436], or even more prosaically the simple requirement, by imitation of the Jews, to wash one's buttocks after the needs![437] These changes in customs were not without resistance: "When they are told 'Follow what God has revealed', they reply: 'No!... We follow the custom of our fathers'"[438]

Then Muhammad turned the Arab laws of vendettas outward. "He advocated and obtained the adoption of measures to avoid the endless chain of vendettas and counter-vendettas. [...] It is implied that no believer shall obstruct, for reasons of kinship or friendship, the accomplishment of justice. [Mohammad, inspired

---

434. *Ibid*, pp. 158-159.
435. See in particular *Le Coran, op. cit.* pp. 172 and 344; HUSSEIN (Mahmoud), *op. cit.* volume I, p. 497.
436. See in particular HICHÂM (Ibn), *op. cit.*, p. 349.
437. See in particular HUSSEIN (Mahmoud), *op. cit.* volume II, p. 188.
438. *The Koran, op. cit.* p. 31.

by Allah, has therefore obtained the adoption of measures for internal peace in the interest of all. [439]

Finally, we find his modifications of laws for personal purposes, which deviated from both the biblical canons and Arab customs. He forbade the dismissal of female believers who had emigrated[440], which was in line with his communitarianism[441]. He encouraged helping orphans, of which he himself had been one[442]. Following the complaint of women who had to marry their husband's heirs against their will, Muhammad received a special law from God to change the Arab custom[443]. For a certain Safwan who complained that his wife's voluntary fasting prevented him from eating when he was hungry, Muhammad invented the law that a wife could not fast without her husband's permission[444]. In general, when we look at Muhammad's personal history, "we relive the circumstances in which multiple verses were revealed to the Prophet, in the very course of his struggle, often in response to an openly expressed expectation on his part, or to pressing questions posed by his companions"[445].

---

439. RODINSON (Maxime), *op. cit.* pp. 186-187.
440. See in particular *The Koran, op. cit.* pp. 689-690.
441. *Ibid,* pp. 135, 430 and 691; HUSSEIN (Mahmud), *op. cit.* volume II, p. 80. The Jews expelled from Medina: RODINSON (Maxime), *op. cit.* p. 226.
442. See in particular *Le Coran, op. cit.* p. 756.
443. See in particular HUSSEIN (Mahmoud), *op. cit.* volume II, pp. 272-273.
444. *Ibid. in* Volume II, p. 400.
445. *Ibid,* Volume II, "Introduction," p. 20.

The example of the famous ban on alcohol is revealing. Muhammad went back and forth three times before finally banning it[446]. The second time, he had a revelation just after one of his companions was too drunk to say the prayer. The prohibition remained partial: "You who believe, do not approach the prayer in a state of drunkenness, not until you know what you are saying..."[447] It wasn't until one of his uncles, who was as round as a shovel, slaughtered innocent camels, that Muhammad banned wine definitively and in all circumstances[448].

In short, Muhammad did not create any law of his own. He distorted those which already existed, either because of contradictions, internal to the Bible or with Arab customs, or for his personal needs according to the vagaries of the context. He had as much difficulty in complying with external laws as he had in imposing on others the generalizations of his personal desires.

We must now try to explain the problems Muhammad had in his relationship to laws, to filiation and to his models of identification.

As a child, Muhammad probably had conflicting relationships with his teachers, whom he must have both loved and hated. Psychologists call this contradictory aspect "drive ambivalence. He must have hated those who did not feed him enough, abandoned him, or even beat him. He was probably reluctant to put up

---

446. See in particular *Le Coran, op. cit.* pp. 41, 100 and 143; HUSSEIN (Mahmoud), *op. cit.* volume II, pp. 23, 209-211.
447. *Ibid*, vol. II, p. 210; *The Qur'an, op. cit.* p. 100.
448. See in particular HUSSEIN (Mahmoud), *op. cit.* volume II, pp. 210-211; *The Koran, op. cit.* p. 143.

with the harsh Arab laws, which must have seen him as the fifth wheel, as an adopted orphan. As we have seen, mercy was not encouraged. The ego of the bullied young Muhammad had to "prefabricate" itself in two: to endure this aggressive world, he escaped into his reveries. He had to talk to himself like Jeliza-Rose, the child heroine of Terry Gilliam's atypical film, *Tideland* (2005), who addresses the heads of four bodiless dolls that she places at her fingertips. The latter has lost her mother, and goes to join her heroin-addicted father in the countryside, who also turns out to be very ill. The real situation turns out to be as unbearable as that of Muhammad as a child.

Freud notes that the early loss of a father, as was the case for Nietzsche, can give rise to a yearning for all that is great and sublime in nature - a mechanism he finds in a text from *Thus Spoke Zarathustra*, "Before Sunrise"[449]. Muhammad must have constituted in his young mind a demanding, elevated "ideal of the self", which the real people around him could only disappoint... Insofar as "... that which does not... kill... strengthens"[450], his personality emerged strengthened, frustrated, but structured, with a solid will and a good reserve of contained aggressiveness, aspiring to rebellion.

---

449. See FREUD (Sigmund), *Psychoanalytical remarks on a case of paranoia (Dementia paranoides) described in autobiographical form* (text entitled "President Schreber") (1910), *in Œuvres complètes. Psychoanalysis*, Paris, PUF, 1993, volume X, p. 277.
450. NIETZSCHE (Friedrich), *op. cit.* volume VIII, "Maxims and traits", § 8, p. 62.

As a young adult, Muhammad married an elderly woman, who was to symbolically relieve him somewhat of his motherlessness. For the time being, he submitted to local customs. But his inability to produce male heirs would be a further frustration for him. These sons would have allowed him to reverse the unfavorable filial relationship of his childhood. His imagination, so sharp, must have appeared to him as a means of refuge during his ascetic isolations, near these distant, idealized beings, which were the prophets of the old books. This terrible aspiration to heaven cost him dearly.

His self cracked. Suddenly, these idealized beings broke into himself. Muhammad identified with them, at least in his revelations. Any reader interested in a story finds himself in the protagonists. Muhammad pushed this normal process to its limits: these biblical characters probably imposed themselves on him as a real second identity. He thought he was them. He felt that he belonged to the family of the prophets. He found an adoptive family, worthy of his demands, outside his clan or the real people who had traumatized his childhood. During these crises, he would literally transport himself into these past stories, or rather he would import them into his mind, which would crack open to make room for them.

How was this second identity nourished? From the religious knowledge that he had gleaned until the age of forty, from the Christians and Jews he had come into contact with, by hearsay. This intruding identity had monopolized all his religious memory, to serve it to him again in the form of a "divine" imperative. He systematically claimed to have to "obey" this voice. Freud would undoubtedly see in it a "super-ego", or "moral conscience", completely detached from his self. These internalized prophets took on independence in Muhammad's mind, and even power over his primary identity. They probably represented his childhood teachers insofar as he loved them, or perhaps would have loved them. They gave him demanding orders.

Later, Muhammad tried to become a symbolic father by giving orders to his contemporaries, whom he unconsciously hated. He tried to replace their customs with the biblical laws of his ideal parents. He loved those who obeyed him, who became the "good ones," and hated those who did not believe in him, the "rebellious" Quraysh. He passed on the love/hate received in childhood to his symbolic descendants, adopted as it were. He had maintained a very problematic hierarchical relationship with his (false) parents. He then had a conflicting relationship with his (false) (adopted) children, namely his (in) subjects. This hatred/love was not yet imposed on the people, and he himself was still subjected to his past educators through their symbolic reincarnation in those prophets who spoke in his ear.

It was only as he gained political power that Muhammad's first identity regained the upper hand. The growing influence on his contemporaries accompanied the reclaiming of his first identity over the second, intruding one. He imperceptibly imposed his biblical laws on his beloved and hated contemporaries, and at the same time his first identity regained the upper hand over the inner intruder, which was used more and more as a pretext to realize his personal desires.

With all these pieces of the puzzle assembled, we are approaching the complete diagnosis of case M. He seems to have achieved the feat of developing a dissociative identity disorder on a particularly paranoid personality. We would then lean towards an exceptional "dissociative paranoia", in other words a paranoia which has integrated as a central delusion a second identity, dissociated from the first. Muhammad's strength must have consisted in building his paranoid system and his social life around this supernumerary identity. He imposed it on his people and ended up imposing himself on them.

We can take a step forward by daring to hypothesize a differential diagnosis, by comparison with the other founders of religion.

In our previous work, we discovered in Jesus a "megaparanoid", in other words a paranoid who invented myths, by so-called "mythical" projections of the structures of his collective unconscious. Muhammad did not invent myths, he simply integrated them into his second identity in order to impose them on his people. On the other hand, he acted concretely, in contrast to Jesus the idealist, whose kingdom was in another world. The diagnosis of the latter could be refined into "megaparanoia of wishful thinking", or idealistic megaparanoia. Where Jesus sublimated, Muhammad enjoyed himself (power, wealth, sex).

To make this comparison between great madmen a little more precise, we could suggest that Muhammad represented a certain regression in relation to Jesus. On the one hand, he stooped to physical aggression, and no longer only symbolic. On the other hand, where Jesus had opened up more universal freedoms, as opposed to a Judaism based on simple cultural customs, Muhammad refocused on very localized laws, such as the use of sand for ablutions, the prohibition of certain foods (alcohol, pork, etc.), codified prohibitions on money, etc. Muhammad also distinguished himself more clearly from other religions and cultures. The latter also distinguished more clearly than his predecessor the bifurcation between love, directed towards the members of the community, and unforgiving hatred, directed towards the "insubordinate". He set himself up as an example of maximum contradiction, having pushed hatred to its extremes (murders, wars, genocides). On the one hand, Muhammad seemed less crazy than Jesus. He did not think he was the son of God, or confused with him. He presented himself as just another prophet. On the other hand, he was much crazier, in that he was extremely violent and imposed his delusions by brute force.

While waiting to analyze Moses in detail one day, we can say that his creativity in delusional entities (Eden, Genesis, etc.) and his political commitment would lead us to hypothesize a "querulous megaparanoia"... if he even existed. Another diagnosis could be applied to Buddha. His personality was marked by depressive phases, a withdrawal from action, and a transposition of his unconscious instances (the ego, the superego, the id) into metaphysical entities (the worldly ego, the eternal Self, vain desires). We would incline to see in him a "sensitive megaparanoid", as a simple research track. These remote diagnoses represent so many provisional suppositions which call for complete studies.

Before we ask how such a personality could have established itself among the people and posterity, let us see again how it unfolded in terms of its claims to be "true" and their relationship to Muhammad's actions. To put it another way, let us examine the truth content of his work and the achievements that should follow from it, in characteristic ways.

CHAPTER SIX
THE PROBLEMATIC KNOWLEDGE OF MUHAMMAD

"You have been given little science."[451]
"The Word, with me, does not change."[452]

Muhammad

How lucky Muhammad was! He possessed what all scientists in the world could only dream of: the exclusive source of absolute knowledge! Let us run to this abundant fountain, whose water remains pure, that is, without contradictions. Let's quickly compare his revealed truth with our present meager knowledge, in order to update it and save ourselves the billions foolishly spent on research.

You can close your eyes and imagine yourself back in school. Open your notebook. Let's start with a light physics lesson, since no experiment is required.

---

451. *The Koran, op. cit.* sura XVII, verse 85, p. 351.
452. *Ibid*, Sura L, verse 29, p. 645.

Right away, we learn that God causes thunder[453], rain[454], wind[455], climate[456], alternating day and night[457]. Astronomy in turn can spare itself tedious observations or costly telescopes[458] : "God raised the firmament's vault; he established it harmoniously; he darkened its night and gave it its brightness."[459] "Have you not seen how God created seven heavens on top of each other? He placed the moon there as a light; he placed the sun there as a lamp."[460] If you were wondering how the sky can remain suspended over our heads, rest assured, you were only missing a little divine trick revealed to Muhammad: "[God] created the heavens without visible pillars; he threw mountains like pillars on the earth so that it would not sway and neither would you [...]"[461] We continue with some basic geology. "God] then stretched out the earth; he brought forth water and pasture from it. He firmly established the mountains for your benefit and that of your flocks."[462] "He made the two seas to meet together; but they do not pass a barrier between them."[463] Demographers will be reassured to learn that the land is large enough to

---

453. *Ibid,* p. 301.
454. *Ibid,* pp. 192, 416 and 436.
455. *Ibid,* p. 626.
456. *Ibid,* p. 436.
457. *Ibid.* at 257 and 436.
458. *Ibid,* pp. 499-500, 650, 706, 719, 743-744.
459. *Ibid,* p. 740.
460. *Ibid,* p. 719.
461. *Ibid,* p. 506.
462. *Ibid,* p. 740.
463. *Ibid,* p. 664.

allow everyone to migrate[464]. In general, Muhammad repeats the fatal error of the Bible, which consists in believing that God made the earth *for* man. Without even mentioning a manifest egocentrism accompanied by immeasurable pride, this belief proves dangerous for nature, which is instrumentalized. It forces man to remain ignorant, since in this system everything is explained in advance. There is no need to understand the vast world by natural causes, it is "explained" by "purposes" - the intentions of God.

Muhammad knew nothing of the scientific process, which proceeds by hypothesis and experimentation, with a view to improving the original conjectures. He thought that "most disbelievers are content with a guess. The assumption does not prevail against the Truth"[465]. Scientists still have to confront their conclusions in order to submit them to criticism, while Muhammad assumed that he had the certain truth, while others remained "...without any science, guidance, or luminous book"[466]. He believed that everything was contained in his book[467] and that the age of a work constitutes a guarantee of its value[468], which undermines the idea of progress attached to science. Finally, modern rationality is accompanied by rules of logic, which did not seem to bother Muhammad. In addition to an extraordinary accumulation of contradictions, which we shall examine below, he was also

---

464. *Ibid*, p. 110.
465. *Ibid*, p. 253. See also pp. 40, 257 and 494.
466. *Ibid*, p. 507.
467. *Ibid*, p. 256.
468. *Ibid*, p. 622.

a man who, in his spare time, indulged in circular reasoning, which is based on what he has to prove: "God [created and harmoniously formed man], and then, from him, he gave birth to a couple: the male and the female. [Would not the one who did this have the power to give life to the dead?][469] In the game of "heads I win, tails you lose", Muhammad taught us that happiness is a sign from God... but so is misfortune[470]. His famous formula *Inch'Allah,* "If God wills it", was in this sense: whatever happens, God wills it! It is like an astrologer saying, "Tomorrow you will win the trifecta, unless you lose. Muhammad was fond of truisms: "The intelligent think." [471]

Let's swallow a truck and give him the opportunity to not bother with the basic rules of how science works. After all, Gabriel was informing him directly. Let's go back to his school, this time in biology class.

Please note, in red: "If any of you is sick; if he suffers from an ailment of the head, he must make amends by fasting [...]"[472] If you doubt that your wife's child is indeed yours, take heart:

"A man came to the Messenger of God and said to him:

- My wife just gave me a black child.
- Don't you have camels from the same camel?
- Yes. A brown color.
- Isn't one of them white?

---

469. *Ibid,* p. 731.
470. *Ibid,* p. 263.
471. *Ibid,* p. 567.
472. *Ibid,* p. 37.

- Yes, it is.

- Where does this color come from?

- Perhaps a deviation of nature.

- Perhaps your son's color is a result of nature's deviation."[473]

We appreciate the "maybe".

In the context of the delicate question of sexual education, one answer will satisfy the most avid of the most refined knowledge:

"Tell us how it can be that a boy looks like his mother, while the liquid comes from the father?

-...] Is it not true that a man's liquid is white and thick, while a woman's liquid is yellow and light? Which of the two prevails determines the likeness."[474]

You move on to the next line, and point out that all living things are sexual: "We have created a pair of each thing"[475], which will allow you to divide the bacteria at the next practice... or not. After birth, let's talk about the dead, who "...endure sufferings that animals can hear"[476], which should not surprise you: "Do not think that those who are killed in the way of God are dead. They are alive!"[477] Indeed, death occurs only when the soul or heart goes up the gullet or collarbone[478]. As much as possible, stay alert. For the next written test,

---

473. HUSSEIN (Mahmoud), *op. cit.* volume II, p. 312.

474. *Ibid*, p. 56.

475. *The Koran, op. cit.* p. 650.

476. HUSSEIN (Mahmoud), *op. cit.* volume II, p. 213.

477. *The Koran, op. cit.* p. 86.

478. *Ibid*, pp. 515, 579, 671 and 730.

note among the constituents of the human body: "It was [God] who created you from clay..."[479]

Regardless of Muhammad's minor errors at times, his general conception of living things suffered from a fundamental flaw. In the current framework of the synthetic theory of evolution, the change in the form of living beings is explained by natural selection and genetic variation, in other words by natural causes. Muhammad, on the other hand, was faithful to the Bible and conceived of living beings as having been created all at once, in their definitive form, for a divine purpose, that of serving man, forgetting in the process that we are unaware of (the existence of) the immense majority of species. The following example abounds in this sense, and also offers us a beautiful lesson in beekeeping: "You get an intoxicating drink and excellent food from the fruits of palms and vines. This is indeed a Sign for a people who understand! Your Lord has revealed to the bees: "Make your homes in the mountains, in the trees and in the hives; then eat of all the fruits. Thus obediently follow the paths of your Lord." From their wombs comes a diaprous liquor from which men find healing. This is indeed a Sign for a thinking people!"[480] Muhammad, in believing that plants and animals are created *to* feed man[481], made research in biology obsolete. The principle was simple. Whenever he wanted to explain a natural fact of which he was fundamentally ignorant,

---

479. *Ibid*, p. 150.
480. *Ibid*, p. 331.
481. *Ibid*, pp. 324, 413 and 719.

he had recourse to God. And, amusingly, he explained everything by God[482].

Freud explains the triple vexation that the humanity had to undergo[483], to go down from its egocentric and dominant conception towards a rational comprehension of the nature: the astronomy of Galileo shows to the man that he is not a master in the center of the universe; the Darwinian revolution makes him understand that he is not either a master in the summit of the life; the psychoanalysis of Freud obliges him to recognize that he is not even the master in his own psyche. As in negative, this triple vexation corresponds to a triple error of the religion, which appears particularly well with the Koran: Muhammad was mistaken on the universe, on the living, and finally misled on the functioning of his own psyche. God did not speak to him, and had created neither the living beings nor the earth in a few days for humanity.

In the human sciences, his ignorance was just as obvious. In psychology, he attributed an oversight to the devil[484]. In sociology, it is still by the mysterious will of God that he explained the life of the peoples[485], the end of the cities[486] or the war victories[487]. In reli-

---

482. *Ibid*, pp. 182, 333, 404, 405, 425, 437 and 617.

483. See FREUD (Sigmund), *Leçons d'introduction à la psychanalyse* (1916-1917), in *Œuvres complètes. Psychanalyse*, Paris, PUF, 2000, tome XIV, lesson XVIII, p. 295; *Les Résistances contre la psychanalyse* (1925), in *Œuvres complètes. Psychoanalysis*, Paris, PUF, 1992, tome XVII, pp. 134-135.

484. See in particular *Le Coran, op. cit.* p. 364.

485. *Ibid.* at 400.

486. *Ibid.* at 414 and 462.

487. *Ibid*, p. 526.

gion, a field in which he was supposed to excel, he showed himself capable of conveying the superstitious myth of the Virgin Mary, absolutely external to Jesus[488]. He took pleasure in inventing quotations that do not appear in the Bible, such as the divinity of Mary[489] or the announcement by Jesus of a prophet to come[490], and triggered legitimate doubts on the part of connoisseurs of the time[491].

Philosophically, things are even worse. Most of the time, he did not present reasons, *since* his truths were "revealed" (he held the science without arguments[492]). He preferred monotheism to polytheism without any evidence[493]. He compared God to other gods among his polytheistic enemies, and praised his supposed exploits by listing all that he is capable of doing, before adding, "Is there any of your associates who is capable of doing this?"[494] Children in the playground talk about their father in the same way. When he made the effort to prove his point, his arguments were beneath everything. He kept repeating that God is the cause of everything[495], the earth[496], the mountains[497], the

---

488. *Ibid*, p. 67.
489. *Ibid*, p. 148.
490. *Ibid*, p. 692.
491. See in particular RODINSON (Maxime), *op. cit.* p. 202.
492. See in particular *Le Coran, op. cit.* p. 509.
493. *Ibid,* pp. 69, 329, 343 and 441.
494. *Ibid*, p. 502.
495. *Ibid,* pp. 129, 252, 299 and 470.
496. *Ibid*, p. 643.
497. *Ibid.*

species[498], the water[499], the plants[500], the harvests[501], the cataclysms[502], the reproduction[503], the deaths[504], the shortages[505], the victories[506], the happiness[507], etc. He produced an extraordinary circular argument, affirming that everything that exists proves the existence of God. For him, everything was a sign[508]. This dream system was fed by projections of human characteristics that were too human. He attributed an intention behind everything real, with useful species[509], the sea[510] and the earth[511] conceived *for* man[512] as "blessings"[513] at his service[514], man placed at the top of the universe[515], astronomy thought in anthropomorphic terms[516], etc. Today, we know the serious ecological consequences of beliefs such as "it is [God] who has made for you the very submissive earth"[517]. This

---

498. *Ibid.*
499. *Ibid*, p. 644.
500. *Ibid.*
501. *Ibid*, p. 188.
502. *Ibid*, p. 191.
503. *Ibid*, p. 192.
504. *Ibid*, p. 194.
505. *Ibid*, p. 198.
506. *Ibid*, p. 213.
507. *Ibid*, p. 216.
508. *Ibid*, pp. 195, 266, 297, 308, 345, 570 and 601.
509. *Ibid.* at 450 and 587.
510. *Ibid*, p. 618.
511. *Ibid*, p. 264.
512. *Ibid*, p. 429.
513. *Ibid*, p. 664.
514. *Ibid*, pp. 324-325.
515. *Ibid*, p. 605.
516. *Ibid*, p. 747.
517. *Ibid*, p. 707.

beautiful system, as fictitious as it was circular, was based on a bottomless pit, since "everything" has a cause, *except* this one cause, God himself. The point of arrival contradicts the point of departure. This is the distressing reasoning of the *causa sui*, the cause of oneself[518]. Nor did he spare us the very weak argument of the richest man in the cemetery: "His wealth and all that he has acquired will be of no use to him"[519], which is tantamount to saying that without God, life has no meaning, *therefore* he exists! Not to mention the fact that this belief puts all philosophers out of work, because we know the meaning of life in advance. Finally, its famous and smoky fatalism[520] generated a characterized bug about free will: "Let him who wills take a way to his Lord; but you will only will if God wills it."[521] If we don't choose, why ask us to convert? Could God condemn people whom he himself has led to do wrong? Muhammad fell headlong into this crude trap: "Your Lord creates what He wills, and He chooses; there is no choice for men."[522]

In a way, we can understand why Muhammad was so sensitive about objections to his system: he must have felt that his so-called knowledge was a collection of dreamlike delusions, so he found it difficult enough to believe it himself without having to face rational criticism. The first to doubt it was himself,

---

518. *Ibid*, p. 50; HUSSEIN (Mahmoud), *op. cit.* volume II, p. 71.
519. HICHAM (Ibn), *op. cit.* p. 123.
520. See in particular *Le Coran, op. cit.* pp. 40, 155, 167, 315, 676, 682, 686 and 691; Rodinson (Maxime), *op. cit.* p. 156.
521. *The Koran, op. cit.* p. 733.
522. *Ibid*, p. 484.

like a dreamer who doubts what he perceives. This lack of self-confidence led to an aggressive tension, all the more so as he based all his life choices, even the meaning of existence, on these unacknowledged errors. Scientific researchers remain serene. They are less hung up on their assertions. They know that any knowledge worthy of the name constitutes a hypothesis that can always be criticized and improved.

If Muhammad had not claimed to know everything, we could not reproach such a lack of science to a quasi-literate[523], who lived in remote times in extreme climatic conditions. But in addition, his so pathological personality could hardly but offer us generous contradictions. These were due in part to his paranoid projections, which led him to reproach others for what he himself was happily doing. At the same time, Muhammad was fond of the obvious discrepancies between his actions and his orders, or more generally his words. His contradictions also arose from the fact that he did not apply the same principles to his submissives as to the "infidels. They also arose from his constant variations of laws, especially from the fact that the commandments of the Bible clashed with each other or departed from Arab customs. A final collection of beautiful inconsistencies concerned his words to each other and their overall coherence - or rather their overall inconsistency.

Let's look at these rich possibilities, with a few crisp examples to liven up the soup.

---

523. See in particular HUSSEIN (Mahmoud), *op. cit.* volume I, p. 12; RODINSON (Maxime), *op. cit.* p. 72.

Now that we are acquainted with the main personality traits of Muhammad, we are able to appreciate to the fullest extent the fact that he reproached his unfortunate contemporaries with hatred[524], malice[525], homicide[526], pride[527], promises to deceive[528], promises of paradise[529], the curious idea of decreeing laws[530], ignorance and insolence[531], passion[532], false arguments and mockery[533], arrogance[534], respect for tradition[535], unjustified violence[536], insults[537], lying[538], stealing[539], misapplication of the Bible[540], fornication[541] (he himself did not fornicate, he married a lot, mind you), etc. It is beautiful of him to have declared:

"Woe to the acerbic slanderer who amasses wealth and counts it!"[542] We keep the icing on the cake: he reproached that one could make reproaches[543]!

---

524. See in particular *The Koran, op. cit.* pp. 77-78.
525. *Ibid,* p. 118.
526. *Ibid,* pp. 10, 16 and 344.
527. *Ibid,* pp. 180, 325, 480, 617, 625 and 727.
528. *Ibid,* p. 348.
529. *Ibid,* p. 330.
530. *Ibid,* p. 338.
531. *Ibid,* p. 345.
532. *Ibid,* p. 359.
533. *Ibid,* p. 363.
534. *Ibid,* p. 507.
535. *Ibid.*
536. *Ibid,* p. 602.
537. *Ibid,* p. 641.
538. See RODINSON (Maxime), *op. cit.* p. 228.
539. See in particular *Le Coran, op. cit.* p. 745.
540. See in particular RODINSON (Maxime), *op. cit.* p. 220.
541. See in particular *Le Coran, op. cit.* p. 344.
542. *Ibid,* p. 767.
543. *Ibid,* p. 53.

We will also be very impressed to learn that Muhammad ordered to tell the truth, he who lied constantly, and to respect justice, he who followed only his own rules, if necessary invented for the occasion. He also urged patience[544], to have only two or three wives[545] (he who married all the beauties he met[546] and who killed a captive to steal his half[547]), to follow the custom[548] and not to innovate[549], not to covet[550], not to commit excesses[551], not to desire other women[552], not to subject oneself to one's passion[553], not to wage war[554], to rise to spirituality[555], not to take revenge for an insult[556], not to seek money[557], not to commit adultery, etc. No doubt he evolved on the subject of wealth, like any good self-respecting upstart: he had to condemn the wealthy and interest loans when he was poor[558], only to deny himself later.

How could the wealthy and powerful Muhammad, married thirteen times, say: "The love of coveted

544. *Ibid,* pp. 29, 81, 263 and 756.
545. *Ibid,* p. 92.
546. See in particular HUSSEIN (Mahmoud), *op. cit.* volume II, p. 51.
547. See in particular RODINSON (Maxime), *op. cit.* p. 289.
548. See in particular *Le Coran, op. cit.* p. 95.
549. See in particular RODINSON (Maxime), *op. cit.* p. 185.
550. See in particular *Le Coran, op. cit.* p. 98.
551. *Ibid,* p. 183.
552. *Ibid,* p. 419.
553. *Ibid,* p. 560.
554. *Ibid,* p. 629; HICHÂM (Ibn), *op. cit.* p. 300.
555. See in particular *The Koran, op. cit.* pp. 730 and 733.
556. HUSSEIN (Mahmoud), *op. cit.* volume II, p. 398.
557. See in particular HICHÂM (Ibn), *op. cit.,* p. 100.
558. See in particular RODINSON (Maxime), *op. cit.* p. 267.

goods is presented to men under beautiful and deceptive appearances; such are the women, the children, the heavy piles of gold and silver, the racy horses, the cattle, the cultivated lands: this is a fleeting enjoyment of the life of this world [...]"[559]? How dare he say to himself, the greatest organizer of raids of his time, that "it is not fitting for a prophet to defraud. Whoever defrauds, will come with his sin on the Day of Resurrection"[560]? He who massacred the Jews because of their susceptibility allowed himself to declare: "Let not hatred towards a people incite you to commit injustice.[561] He who converted people by threat, interest and force, quietly declared: "Whoever remains a Jew or a Christian cannot be forced to leave his religion"[562], or more briefly: "No compulsion in religion!"[563] How could he condemn lending at interest on the one hand, while on the other hand he said: "To him who makes a good loan, God will repay it abundantly"[564]? Muhammad also gave us the superb case of the burnt palm trees, which earned him the lucid reproaches of his contemporaries: "You who used to blame and forbid the destruction of property, why do you cut down and burn our palm trees?"[565]

---

559. *The Koran, op. cit.* p. 61.

560. *Ibid*, p. 84.

561. *Ibid*, p. 127.

562. HICHÂM (Ibn), *op. cit.* p. 391.

563. *The Koran, op. cit.* p. 51. See also HUSSEIN (Mahmoud), *op. cit.* volume II, p. 22.

564. *The Koran, op. cit.* p. 48. See also HUSSEIN (Mahmoud), *op. cit.* volume II, p. 76.

565. HICHÂM (Ibn), *op. cit.* p. 257. See also Rodinson (Maxime), *op. cit.* p. 226.

Muhammad also contradicted his words in general by his actions. He who was so lecherous and greedy, as a good paranoid who found no fault with himself, said without shame: "God has not commanded me to amass the treasures of the world, nor to satisfy all my appetites. [... So I do not hoard dinar or dirham and I do not withhold any gift until the next day.[566] He called himself a scholar[567] and asked for proof from others[568]. Fortunately, he said: "To say what you do not do is greatly hated by God![569] His inconsistent fatalism gave him the opportunity for a beautiful blunder: "If your Lord had wanted it, all the inhabitants of the earth would have believed. Is it for you to force men to believe, when it is not for anyone to believe without God's permission?[570] One might think that this was a severe criticism of Muhammad.

He also contradicted himself according to the people to whom his laws applied, who were divided into three clearly differentiated categories: the "insubordinate"; his community of submissives; and his own modest self. The words *equality* and *universality probably did* not exist in the Arabic vocabulary of the time. In the Qur'an, Muhammad constantly balanced between a vengeful and a forgiving God[571], thus creating a striking contrast between a vengeful God[572], who

---

566. HUSSEIN (Mahmoud), *op. cit.* volume II, p. 37.
567. See especially *The Koran, op. cit.* pp. 463 and 496.
568. *Ibid*, p. 622.
569. *Ibid*, p. 691.
570. *Ibid*, p. 262.
571. *Ibid*, pp. 4, 32, 33, 36 and 634.
572. *Ibid*, p. 199.

aids in massacres[573], who authorizes killing[574], and the ever-repeating formula of the "merciful God", who ensures happiness within the 'Umma[575]. He solved this problem brutally: "God returns unceasingly to the repentant sinner; he is merciful. [But there is no forgiveness for those who do wrong..."[576] Alas, there is a double standard, as he liked to reproach[577], in that only some could break the laws: "Mohammad began to cut down the palm trees of the Nadiri. But a revelation from Allah confirmed that the prophet's military behavior was right.[578] The key to these beautiful contradictions between words and deeds lies in the fact that he achieved the feat of believing that his injustices were just, since God authorized them, hence a splendid asymmetry for the same acts: "The recourse [to retaliation] is possible only against those who are unjust to men and who, without reason, show themselves violent on the earth. These are the ones who will suffer a painful punishment.[579] Muhammad was accustomed to the privileged rights that God granted him personally, as in the case of his relationship with women[580]. His jealousy made him rule (by God, of course) that no one could marry his former wives[581]. How could he claim to have a universal message and

---

573. *Ibid,* pp. 79 and 84.

574. *Ibid,* p. 108.

575. *Ibid,* p. 75.

576. *Ibid,* p. 95.

577. *Ibid,* p. 276.

578. RODINSON (Maxime), *op. cit.* p. 226.

579. *The Koran, op. cit.* p. 602.

580. *Ibid,* p. 521.

581. *Ibid,* p. 522.

to impose himself on the rest of the world, when his revelations were imbued with the Arab context (such as washing with sand) or autobiographical (such as the laws for his own wives, he the last of the prophets)?

The political leader Muhammad spent his time inventing tailor-made, opportunistic laws, a pale mixture of local culture and contingent arrangements (as we saw in chapter VI). Not surprisingly, they contradict each other. He went back and forth before resolutely banning alcohol[582]. He could encourage pride when it was in his interest to do so, as in the case of one of his fighters who strutted around with the sword lent to him by Muhammad to incite war: "This is a step God does not like, except in a situation such as ours."[583] In his hesitant early days, he admitted other deities[584]. He often contradicted previous laws[585], in all conscience. Some people asked him, "How can Muhammad command his companions to do something that he later forbids them, and then command them to do something else? How can he say today what he will deny tomorrow? So this Qur'an is only the word of Muhammad, words that emanate only from him and contradict each other." Then the Most High revealed, "As soon as we abrogate a verse or erase it from memory, we bring another, better or similar.""[586] Current scholars comment: "One question

---

582. See HUSSEIN (Mahmoud), *op. cit.* volume II, pp. 210-211.
583. HICHÂM (Ibn), *op. cit.* p. 238.
584. See in particular RODINSON (Maxime), *op. cit.* p. 124.
585. See in particular HUSSEIN (Mahmoud), *op. cit.* volume II, p. 375.
586. *Ibid,* pp. 109-110; *The Qur'an, op. cit,* p. 20.

that has been constantly on people's minds is which verses of the Qur'an have been abrogated by later revelations. The fact is indisputable, since it is mentioned in the Koran. But the problem is this: between two disputed verses, it is not always clear which one came down last - and therefore which one is to be considered abrogating and which one abrogated.[587] We might ask again: if Muhammad had lived longer, would he not have changed his mind again? Would God hesitate? "Allah repeated his revelations, added to them and changed them. The opponents would point this out in an unkind way. But Allah replied that he was free to do what he wanted and also to modify his message.[588] What a coincidence that these rectifications always abounded in the direction of the momentary interests of their humble receiver!

Muhammad made contradictions between his own words. "God is powerful over all things"[589], however "Creator of the heavens and the earth, how can he have a child, when he has no companion, when he has created everything and knows everything?"[590]

To promote disinterestedness, he found nothing better than a bargain for our benefit: "Say, 'I do not ask you for any wages for this, except your affection for your relatives.'" To him who does a beautiful deed, we will respond with something even more beautiful. God is the one who forgives and he is grateful."[591]

---

587. HUSSEIN (Mahmoud), *op. cit.* volume I, p. 24.
588. RODINSON (Maxime), *op. cit.* p. 161.
589. *The Koran, op. cit.* p. 533.
590. *Ibid,* pp. 122 and 166.
591. *Ibid,* p. 600.

Maxime Rodinson rightly notes, "Here we can already feel the contradiction between the human aspiration to salvation that the prophets and founders of religion are led to understand as a reward and the moral sentiment that has long denied any merit to what is done for a selfish purpose."[592]

If "Your Lord is the one who is self-sufficient [...]"[593], why did he create us?

Muhammad also gave us the gift of a confusion between morality and justice, which was at the origin of the disastrous mixing of religion and politics, between the good and the just: "These are the laws of God; do not transgress them. Those who transgress the laws of God are unjust."[594]

The scholars note that there is a great deal of confusion on the sensitive subject of the status of women: "Muhammad is trying to reduce the distance between the status of women in the Qur'an in the hereafter and the social status he assigns to them during their earthly existence. From an eschatological perspective, the status of women is equal to that of men, since they, like men, are personally accountable to God on the Day of Judgment, and will be individually punished and deserve either Hell or Paradise. As far as the temporal plan is concerned, the Qur'an confirms the place of women in the context of the time. She is then, in relation to her father and husband, in the

---

592. RODINSON (Maxime), *op. cit.* p. 156.
593. *The Koran, op. cit.* p. 171.
594. *Ibid*, p. 44.

relationship of inferiority characteristic of patriarchal society, in Arabia as in the rest of the world"[595]

The case of the copyist 'Abdallah ibn Sa'd, who took the revelations of Muhammad under dictation, and who was able to change the words without the author finding fault with them, leaves a clear uneasiness[596].

For the sake of argument, we will note a fundamental contradiction between what he forbade on earth and promised in heaven. How could Muhammad endlessly promise money and women in heaven when he condemned them on earth? Why should we wear a belt for a lifetime and then take off our pants for good? Pascal's wager[597] is challenged: our present limited life of immoral enjoyment would be a nothingness to be sacrificed in the face of an eternity of happiness to be gained, but if the latter does not exist, our life in turn becomes infinite in comparison to the nothingness that follows. But the balance is tipped in favor of our present pleasures if we take into account the fact that they are certain, very real, while paradise remains at least uncertain. The reversal is complete when one realizes that Paradise only amplifies the beautiful earthly pleasures. To condemn the latter in order to better enjoy them later on appears as the supreme contradiction.

Let us close this firework of contradictions with a final bouquet: "Do they not meditate on the Koran?

---

595. HUSSEIN (Mahmoud), *op. cit.* volume II, pp. 16-17.
596. See in particular RODINSON (Maxime), *op. cit.* p. 253.
597. See *Pensées*, in *Œuvres complètes*, Paris, Éditions du Seuil, 1963, p. 591.

If it came from someone other than God, they would find many contradictions in it."[598]

Can we forgive everything, even a very sick person?

If his case begins to appear clearly to us, a mystery has thickened: how could a being so ignorant, incoherent, fundamentally aggressive and suffering from a serious dysfunction of double identity have convinced and then united a brawling people, and beyond that enthused hundreds of millions of men? To put it even more crudely: how can we understand that countless generations have tried to conform to arbitrary and contradictory laws, not respected by their author, who had taken them from vague memories and distorted them according to his daily needs?

---

598. *The Koran, op. cit.* p. 106.

CHAPTER SEVEN
THE SUBMISSION OF THE PEOPLE
AND POSTERITY

Opposite Muhammad, this hardly believable character, were equally astonishing people, but for quite different reasons. Let us begin by looking at their reactions to the appearance of a dissociative paranoid. We have seen that their first reflex was, in majority, a movement of rejection and incomprehension, followed by accusations of insanity. Until then, this was understandable. But how, afterwards, was a minority convinced, to become a majority and finally an almost unanimous crowd?

To begin with, among the Meccans there were only "...a few men, not more than twenty, who could read and write..."[599]. If Muhammad had an imprecise knowledge of the Bible, few people around him were able to verify it.

It was first the simple-minded or weak-minded who joined Muhammad: "The Senate (the *mala'*, the name

---

599. HUSSEIN (Mahmoud), *op. cit.* volume I, p. 449.

of the Council of Elders in Mecca), the ungrateful of his people replied: 'We see in you only a man like us, and we see among your followers only the vilest of us, the brainless.'"[600] "The people around him were naive and ignorant"[601] ; "[...] there were men and women, among the most vulnerable, who believed early in God and His Prophet"[602]. We recognize here the same process as Jesus did with the poor, or the Muslim Brothers with the disenfranchised. "The humble of condition or spirit like Khabbâb or Bilâl held the modest, but indispensable, job of simple faithful, of "basic" adherents as we would say. Their untiring devotion, their total abnegation, their absolute lack of curiosity and anxiety, in addition to the invaluable material services they rendered, made them models to propose to opponents and disputants."[603]

This low status among an already disadvantaged people makes it possible to understand the incredible credulity that some of his relatives could show, as the following story shows: "[Muhammad] went out to harangue his men: 'Every man of you, I swear, who fights today against the Quraysh and dies bravely, facing them, will enter Paradise.'" On hearing this promise, 'Umayr ibn al-Humâm, who was eating some dates he had in his hand, exclaimed with joy, "Bakh! Bakh! Would there be nothing between Paradise and me but my death at the hands of these

---

600. RODINSON (Maxime), *op. cit.* p. 131.
601. HUSSEIN (Mahmoud), *op. cit.* volume I, p. 338.
602. *Ibid. in* Volume I, p. 339.
603. RODINSON (Maxime), *op. cit.* p. 160.

people?" He threw away his dates, grabbed his sword and launched himself at the Quraysh. He fought them to the death."[604]

In his early days in Medina, as much as the rabbis were suspicious of his knowledge, his early followers were mostly interested in laws: "The Muslims, for their part, asked a few questions about what was permissible and what was not."[605]

Let's take the example of the birth of the famous call to prayer, typical of the Muslim world[606]. Muhammad was looking for a way to synchronize Muslims for prayer. "Then 'Abd Allâh ibn Zayd al-Ansâri had a dream, which he came to tell the Messenger of God: "I saw a man standing on the wall of the Mosque. He made a call to prayer, which he repeated once before sitting down. After a while, he stood up and repeated his double call, adding these words: 'The prayer begins, the prayer begins!'" The Messenger of God said, "You have had a happy vision. Teach the formula to Bilâl. This is how he will call for prayer.[607] A little anecdote: on hearing this cry, the infidels came to Muhammad and said, "How can you accept this cry, which is like that of a camel? There is nothing uglier or coarser"[608], and he was offended: "They consider your call to prayer as a mockery and a game. This is so because they are people who do not understand.[609]

---

604. HICHÂM (Ibn), *op. cit.* pp. 203-204 and 233.
605. *Ibid*, p. 183.
606. *Ibid*, pp. 182-183.
607. HUSSEIN (Mahmoud), *op. cit.* volume II, pp. 86-87.
608. *Ibid*, p. 87.
609. *The Koran, op. cit.* p. 137.

Once this rite was instituted, countless generations would imitate it without ever having the idea of criticizing it.

We are dealing here with a phenomenon of deep humanity, as a gregarious species, which consists in imitating each other, in act. One day, Muhammad was trying to have a ritual of camel slaughter performed, but his mere words did not lead to obedience... " Umm Salama suggested to him, "Start by performing the ritual yourself, they will do it after you." He followed her advice. [...] The Muslims hurried to follow his example. They all rushed together on the camels, so much so that I feared they would fall on top of each other and choke."[610] This last point is reminiscent of the deadly mobs of the current pilgrimages to Mecca.

This mechanism of example in action is especially true if a person presents himself with certainty and threats. "Urwa [a Quraysh representative] saw for himself the conduct of the Prophet's companions: if he performed ablutions, they all rushed to do so; if he spat, they all spat; if a hair fell from his head, they rushed to pick it up...."[611] We then agree with this analysis: "[...] Muhammad kept telling his people, "I am a human being like you, who sometimes makes mistakes like you." But his words, deeds and actions were to be taken as references by all Muslims after his death. They were to constitute the second source of science in Islam, after the Qur'an, and were in turn written down, discussed, set up as norms, and even

---

610. HUSSEIN (Mahmoud), *op. cit.* volume II, pp. 428-429.
611. HICHÂM (Ibn), *op. cit.* p. 303.

sacralized by some."[612] It is in this sense that a host of rituals were born simply from the imitation of Muhammad, such as the pilgrimage with its rules, its different stations and its complete ceremonial[613], the way of doing ablutions[614], the sharing of the booty[615], the purification by the sand[616], the way of sacrificing cattle at the Temple[617], the number of prayers per day[618], their direction[619], etc.

The repetition of the verses of the Koran, preferably dozens of times a day, produced a remarkable effect on his listeners: "These returns of the idea and the verb, these assonances, these refrains obsess, bring the listener himself closer to a hypnotic state (Max Estman), hallucinated, where he will receive, tenfold, as in a state of trance himself, the suggestion of the verb, of the rhythm, of the images."[620]

As for the trances of Muhammad, the people of the time could not understand them. We have seen the complexity of his case, which requires to be understood the whole psychological arsenal of a century of clinical research. If men knew how to say "I don't know" when they can't explain something, would superstitions and religions still exist? They are

---

612. HUSSEIN (Mahmoud), *op. cit.* volume I, p. 21.
613. See in particular HICHÂM (Ibn), *op. cit.*, p. 396.
614. See in particular HUSSEIN (Mahmoud), *op. cit.* volume I, p. 315.
615. See in particular HICHÂM (Ibn), *op. cit.*, p. 280.
616. *Ibid,* p. 100.
617. *Ibid,* p. 309.
618. *Ibid,* p. 85; HUSSEIN (Mahmoud), *op. cit,* volume I, p. 316.
619. *Ibid. in* Volume II, p. 109.
620. RODINSON (Maxime), *op. cit.* p. 124.

so afraid of the unknown that they prefer to explain everything at all costs, even if it means lying to themselves, inventing ridiculous entities, magical mechanisms, and creating monumental illusions.

After convincing the weak-minded, gaining power from their coming together, and overthrowing the strong-minded but isolated, Muhammad obtained a new social configuration: uniting under his banner brought more benefits than opposing his delusions. In particular, the share of the spoils to be gleaned and the fear of being beaten in case of resistance appeared to be the most convincing of divine arguments.

Another deep trait of gregarious humanity is essential to place a simple man on a pedestal. People have a visceral need to admire. They seem to crave models to guide them through life. Rather than taking the personal risk of choosing values for themselves, most people are content to blindly follow inherited norms. As a result, the person who embodies the values of the people is idealized to an extraordinary degree. The image that people have of him or her is totally out of step with the everyday person. Today, many TV presenters, rock stars, top athletes and politicians can be adored by the masses, while they are consumed by their oversized egos, fueled by a boundless vanity. The discrepancy between their self-esteem and the enormous pressure of popular expectation is all too often resolved by taking massive amounts of confidence-boosting drugs or forgetting oneself. But people ignore this aspect and prefer to project their ideals on these embodied supports.

In Jesus, we discovered an immense gap between the real man and the image that Christians have of him[621]. This gap increases with time, forgetting more and more the original case. From then on, recalling the prosaic reality of the latter ends up appearing "blasphemous" - a gesture which consists in passing from the illusory support of a sacralized ideal to the simple existence of a man. No doubt the latter possesses exceptional character traits, but rarely in the way we would expect. By dint of accumulating the needs of admiration of the peoples during centuries, Muhammad also ends up passing for a quasi living god. Do we need to remind ourselves of the values and morals implicitly approved in the Koran and in Muhammad's actions? - Communitarianism, anti-Judaism, sexism, (state) lies, slavery, corporal punishment, the instrumentalization of nature for human comfort, the subordination of politics to religion, spiritual and scientific intolerance, tyranny (in the name of an absolute and divine truth, with the elimination of divergent ways), robbery in organized gangs (or "razzia"), assassination (ordered against opponents of the faith), terrorism (conversion by threat and force), war, genocide, torture, pedophilia, incest (between cousins at least), rape (of captives), greed for power, money and sex, etc.

Let us now sketch a hypothesis on the balance of power obtained between Muhammad and his submissives. On the one hand, we had a people who lived in extreme conditions, not very knowledgeable, without

---

621. See in particular JOI (Frédéric), *op. cit.* p. 191.

unified direction, superstitious, eager for rituals and ideal models to imitate, gregarious, credulous, comprising as everywhere on earth beautiful village idiots, very infantile as for their thirst for obedience, naturally fearing the blows, having interest to unite in spite of an unmanageable aggressiveness within the framework of the clan laws, without counting its visceral need, common to all the human ones, to explain the world, even if it means believing the first far-fetched speculation come.

On the other side, we had a strong personality, hyper aggressive, with inexplicable crises, capable of high poetry, very charismatic, repeating again and again the same ideas with an uncommon stubbornness, producing physical as well as metaphysical threats, using his anal character to make political calculations that were too efficient, eliminating opponents, silencing the rare scholars, finding himself impossible to refute, deploying an extraordinary energy, diverting the aggressiveness and the clan rules of his followers towards scapegoats outside the community, also turning this hatred against the individuals themselves by bad conscience, channelling this aggressiveness by obsessive rituals, containing it moreover by his own ferocity, practising very virulent encouragements of troops, delegating his power to subordinates[622] to widen his control, etc.

Between the two, we found a very simple system of global explanation of the world that allowed to

---

622. See in particular HUSSEIN (Mahmud), *op. cit.* volume II, pp. 100 and 282; HICHAM (Ibn), *op. cit.* pp. 88, 251 and 254.

establish its power on appearances of absolutes, made up of mega-projections that had already proved themselves, coming from the collective unconscious of the previous prophets, such as the creation of the universe with a purpose, the father's anger, his forgiveness and his love, the promised paradise as the end of internal psychological tensions, eternity as the exit of time from consciousness, etc.

We were witnessing a new marriage between madmen[623], with the political dimension in addition. The submissive gave the keys of their own jail to their tyrant. The meeting of Muhammad and the Arabs gave rise to a direct theocracy, which confused law, politics, ethics and religion, while blocking in advance any opening towards new truths. It was a closed, definitive system, a crucible for many aggressive dictatorships to come.

The joy of obtaining a new unity had undoubtedly to make forget this disadvantage. By combining their forces, the Arabs were gratified to be able to conquer new lands. The sad logic of tyranny called its sister conquest.

This forced unity could not last forever, especially because of the many initial contradictions. Should the submissive refer to the deeds or words of Muhammad? And what acts or words? Moreover, some Muslims were ashamed of some of his "deeds", such as paedophilia, which they found it more appropriate to deny outright. Schisms and clan logic came back to crack this unexpected unity.

---

623. JOI (Frédéric), *op. cit.* pp. 167 ff.

In any case, the enormous weight of sheepish habits, the collective hypnosis by a bewitching poetry, the sacralization of a man set up as an absolute model by visceral need of veneration and the revealing tension on the truth of his words generated an immense posterity which crossed the centuries. We will not see the end of it until an education in science and a little material comfort raise the level of the masses.

CONCLUSION

We can pose the general hypothesis that mystical and religious phenomena derive from extreme experiments carried out on the functioning of the brain, as the site of the relationship between the mind and the body. The techniques used are diverse: undernourishment, over or under oxygenation, extreme concentration, very demanding physical exercises, mental pathologies such as psychosis or dissociative disorders, hypnosis, trances, intoxication by hallucinogenic or other substances, taking of drugs in general (from simple coffee, tea, cannabis or alcohol in excessive doses, to poppy or coca leaf derivatives, etc.).

In these secondary states, which we would call pathological, these limit experimenters access other types of thoughts. They hallucinate, reach dreamlike states, make megaprojections, plunge deeply into themselves, trigger acute artificial psychoses, feel their bodies and the world intensely by disconnecting intellectual consciousness, etc. They disturb the functioning of their mind so much that the psychologist has a lot of work to do in order to find the right sources for them. They disturb so much the functioning of their mind that the psychologist has a lot of work to do to find the real sources of their delusions and to put some order in them.

After having turned their heads, they try to give an account of what they have seen or felt, this time with the intellect, to share it. Very often, they interpret these states, visions and other auditory hallucinations from the hypothesis of parallel worlds, supernatural entities, unreal mechanisms, etc. The complexity of a single human brain is such that it is capable of harboring several independent identities, voices or characters that can express themselves with varying degrees of autonomy from the main "I", if given the opportunity.

These mystics give more or less credence to what they have seen, and attribute to it this or that degree of reality. In the best of cases, they draw from it concrete instructions to live their daily life more positively, to breathe better, to know themselves more intrinsically, to brood less in vain, etc. In the worst case, they get hammered into their heads, think they are living gods or prophets, and then aggressively correct the behaviors and beliefs of their contemporaries. The most convinced, the most convincing, the most aggressive, the most inspired manage to galvanize their entourage with the interpretation they have made of their internal states... From then on, common beliefs, collective rites, sects, religions are born.

Such was undoubtedly Muhammad. By dint of his limitations, of eating little, of isolating himself, of being frustrated, etc., his conscience cracked, giving way to a character other than himself, who borrowed his own knowledge of religion. When this internal stranger appeared, Muhammad greeted him with caution. Then he let him express himself, at first entirely. He was overwhelmed by his rebellious unconscious. Later, when success and confidence came, Muhammad regained control over this internal host. He put it at the service of his aggressiveness, his inclinations for money, power and sex.

In the remote times when these "mystics" and "prophets" were delirious, scientific psychology did not exist. The gullible people accepted the interpretation that they made of their states, as superior manifestations, of another world, of several deities or of only one god. Today, psychologists explain these states from the unconscious. This is the case for the president of a court of assizes, a certain Schreber, who thought he had woven a special link with God, from threads that in fact represented his own impulses[624]. He believed that if he was not impregnated by God, the world would disappear. He projected the fact that if a subject no longer attaches himself to reality by means of the impulse links, the world disappears in his eyes. This president was committed to a psychiatric hospital, and Freud tried afterwards to understand his case. In the same way, when certain people do not control themselves any more, when spectacular crises deprive them of the control of their limbs, of their ideas or of whole parts of their identity, the

---

624. See FREUD (Sigmund), *op. cit.* volume X.

modern Westerners call upon the psychiatrists. They then speak of hysteria, dissociative disorders, or frank schizophrenia. Scientific understanding has replaced religious interpretation.

In this sense, Muhammad appears to us as a severe and very rare case of dissociative querulous paranoia. In his time, he had to deal with the fact that specialized hospitals did not yet exist. His high level of aggressiveness and his very organized character met with the ignorance, fear and finally submission of his contemporaries. He was able to impose his delusion on them and even use it to satisfy his desires - all too human.

We can summarize these hypotheses with the help of the following table. This one presents the course of Muhammad, such as we tried to reconstitute it starting from the historical documents which indirectly reveal his uncommon psychological operation, and his insertion in the social framework. The arrows indicate the direction of the psychological and social pressures.

Periods People in attendance	(Young) child	Adolescent and young adult	Quadragenarian (from the revelations)	Fifty years old (from the hegira)	Posthumous
Main identity (Muhammad)	Analogue character set up; lack of parents	Poorly developed paranoia that integrates smoothly into society through trade and marriage; lack of male children	Querulous paranoia with delusions of filiation that clashes with the community; Muhammad submits to the revealed message and tries in vain to impose it	Querulous dissociative paranoia with hyperaggressivity: Muhammad imposes his voice and imposes himself on her ↓	The caliph or head of state takes over and replaces Muhammad; he submits to the message, imposes it on the people (and the world)
Secondary identity (Gabriel)	Imaginary universe to take refuge in	The second identity simmers while Muhammad assimilates rough biblical knowledge	↑ States of dissociative trance; Gabriel appears and imposes himself; identity constructed from biblical knowledge; source of doubt then of certainty for Muhammad	Gabriel is tamed and put at the service of the first identity ↓	The Koran acts as a source of absolute but contradictory knowledge ↓
Arab Community	↑ High pressure; hungry (and possibly abused) orphan	= Adaptation, financial and family integration; balance between Muhammad and his society	↑ Refusal of his clan; Muhammad forced to flee (cave, group in Abyssinia, oasis of Taif, then Medina)	The Arabs submit and unify little by little	Arabs are submissive and unified on one side; but contradict each other on the other (schisms and cultural differences) ↓
	The Arabs are divided into clans; vendettas and razzias				
Other communities and the rest of the world		Muhammad learns from the Jews and Christians	Muhammad tries in vain to impose Judeo-Christianity	↑Then↓ support from the Jews; then rejection by Muhammad	Wars of conquest to all non-Muslims

CONCLUSION

One of the most sensitive aspects of this encounter between a dissociative paranoid querulous and a submissive people concerns the relationship between certainty and tyranny. Insofar as Muhammad believed that he held truths directly from heaven, we can see that tyranny begins with certainty. That it then meets with an absence of criticism, and its rule is assured for a long time. Just the opposite presides over the functioning of democracy: like science, it relies on hypotheses that are always subject to collective criticism and objective tests, with a view to progressive improvements. Religion poses certainties disconnected from reality, which it fixes and imposes on the people, who are alienated in a collective psychosis. To liberate this one, we count on the Lights of the reason, acquired by a specific education.

Muhammad channeled aggression by diverting it onto "others" and the individual himself (the guilty conscience before God), crushing it under violence and enshrining it in rituals. But the best solution to manage aggressiveness, sublimation, is not used at all. And for good reason: Muhammad himself largely abandoned it. It consists in raising one's impulses towards symbolic goals, useful to society. The education of the people allows to turn them towards abstract ideas. We think that humanity must rise from infantile beliefs to adult knowledge. Religion locks man into a dream where a supreme father would watch over everything and provide in advance for all his desires.

We certainly do not call for any war against religions, which would amount to falling into what we denounce, the primary use of unsublimated impulses. On the contrary, we would like to take advantage of their legitimate quest for meaning and transform it into an effort to understand the world, to adapt ourselves harmoniously to it. We call humanity to an inner war, in view of an elevation towards reason. We call for the high noon, where the shadow of error is the shortest[625].

625. See NIETZSCHE (Friedrich), *op. cit*, "How, in the end, the 'True World' became a fable. History of a mistake", p. 81.

RECREATION:
TEST YOUR SUBMISSION SKILLS

You will have understood that Muhammad demands your submission. You will also have understood that, even with the best will in the world, following his convoluted injunctions is not easy. It is a problem.

To solve this problem, we have designed this test especially for you. It will allow you to know right now if you deserve paradise, by being as faithful as possible to the truths revealed in the Koran.

Don't miss it. Eternity in hell is long, especially towards the end.

Question 1:

At what age did you discover to your amazement that your parents were not perfect?

    A - from childhood ;

    B - in adolescence;

    C - what? My parents are perfect.

Question 2:

Knowing that Muhammad said "...do not be among those...who have divided their religion and formed sects, each faction rejoicing in what it has"[626]:

A - you return to the original Islam, leaving Sunnism, Shiism, Kharidjism and other currents, even if you feel quite alone;

B - you follow both Sunnism, in its variants Hanafite, Malekite, Shafiite, Salafist Hanbalite, Wahabi Hanbalite, etc., Shiism, in its Imamite or Duodeciman, Zaydite, Alawite Ismaili, Nizarite Ismaili, Druze Ismaili, Alevist, Kaysanite, etc. versions, Ibadite and Mozabite Kharidjism, Mutazilism, Sufism, Mortabitism, etc, by accepting and not accepting the marriage of pleasure (abolished by Omar), by authorizing and not authorizing the representations of Muhammad, by imposing and not imposing the niqab (which shows only the eyes), by practicing and not practicing asceticism, by following Abû Bakr and Ali, by praying three times and five times a day, by dissimulating (*takiya*) and not dissimulating your faith in a hostile environment, performing and not performing the rite of Ashura, replacing and not replacing the great pilgrimage to Mecca (*Haj*) with visiting the tombs of the Imams (*ziyara*), hitting and not hitting your wife, forbidding and not forbidding music, cutting and not cutting the hand of

---

626. *The Koran, op. cit.* p. 501.

thieves, considering the Imams as fallible and infallible, doing and not doing the Tarawih prayer in the mosque during Ramadan, etc.:

C - you drop the contradictions of Muhammad and the currents that claim to him. You join a petanque club, the rules are simpler.

Question 3:

If Muhammad tells you that there are seven heavens and that the sun is a lamp that God has hung there[627], while the present astronomers show you that the universe is expanding and that the earth turns on itself:

A - you interpret the seven heavens as a metaphor, without really knowing what ;

B - you go to war (*jihad*) against astronomers;

C - you're kidding.

Question 4:

A verse deliberately left unspoken by the Imams states: "It is better to prostrate oneself before the Lord twenty-two times a day than to forget one of the five prayers prescribed by Him; the insubordinate will taste the boiling water of eternal Hell"[628]:

A - you start right away to have time to finish before tomorrow;

B - you use your mobile to program five ring tones and never forget the five prescribed prayers;

C - you replace genuflections with yoga, it's better for your health, especially mental.

---

627. *Ibid*, p. 719.
628. *Ibid*, p. 773, Sura CXV, verse 11.

Question 5:

Knowing that Muhammad married thirteen times while ordering: "Marry, as you please, two, three or four women"[629] :

> A - you will contract up to four marriages, as he said;
>
> B - you will contract eight and a half marriages, in doubt ;
>
> C - you will choose in your soul and conscience what will happen in your life, in accordance with the laws of your country.

Question 6:

Muhammad commanded, "Fight in the way of God."[630] If you are not currently practicing *jihad* (struggle, effort) with the sword... :

> A - you consider that the other forms of *jihad,* by the heart, the tongue and the hand, appear more satisfactory in the eyes of God;
>
> B - you think that Muhammad may have made a slight error of appreciation of human psychology, the truth is not imposed with a sword;
>
> C - you consider that you have lacked courage so far, but intend to get your act together soon and blow up the White House, which will undoubtedly help to convert the Americans, those unforgivable infidels.

---

629. *Ibid,* p. 92.
630. *Ibid,* p. 48.

Question 7:

Is Jesus the son of God?

- A - what's wrong with that? God is powerless to do such a thing;
- B - yes, but indirectly, by *in vitro* fertilization, God is all-powerful and very clever;
- C - no, Jesus is the son of Joseph, who discreetly deflowered Mary while she was sleeping, she did not realize anything.

Question 8:

Muhammad claimed to be a man like any other and as such he could be wrong[631]... You think that :

- A - this is one of the few times he was right;
- B - he was nevertheless the only one who held the truth; you must obey his divine words and imitate his actions;
- C - he was only mistaken on this point, so much he exceeded infinitely all the other men.

Question 9:

Muhammad claims that man comes from God. Darwin claims that he descended from the monkey. Your opinion:

- A - Genesis is a mere metaphor. It doesn't matter if you don't know exactly what it is;
- B - only Darwin descends from the monkey to be able to invent such a theory;
- C - when you don't know something, you should have the courage to say "I don't know".

---

631. See HUSSEIN (Mahmoud), *op. cit.* volume I, p. 21.

Question 10:

Can you change your mind as often as the Prophet did, for example about drinking alcohol?

> A - yes, and even more; to please Muhammad, you will decide not to consume alcohol for a decade, then rinse your tonsils for ten years, stop again for a decade, and go on a last bender before drinking the water of paradise for eternity;
>
> B - you will drink reasonably from time to time by making the effort (*jihad*) to cultivate an extraordinary faculty of your mind: free will;
>
> C - you will trust the Imams to choose the last revelation of Gabriel on this and that subject.

Question 11:

If a new prophet comes along and says that you should believe in Moses, Jesus and Muhammad, but also beware of imitators because he is the last of the prophets, what do you do?

> A - you follow this last prophet who said that he would be the last one, and you go to war against these unbelievers of Jews, Christians and Muslims who do not want to believe in this new messenger of God;
>
> B - you hesitate; you prefer the original to the copy, but you are not sure where the original lies;
>
> C - you drop those prophets who imitate and contradict each other, and you make your reason work to decide your life.

Question 12:

Muhammad did not impose the *hijab* ("veil") on the face of women[632]. You think that :

    A - women are equal to men, they are free to dress as they please, especially since they usually do so with more taste. Granting freedom to women is enough to see that in addition to their ability to reproduce and give birth, they are capable of thinking, driving, studying, running businesses, assuming political responsibilities, etc. ;

    B - to avoid making waves, you discreetly mingle with the sheep of your country by following their customs, whatever their nature and origin, and you learn to pronounce "bêêêê" without an accent;

    C - it is to honor Muhammad to magnify his initial intention with this scarf, and for this purpose you develop a kind of walking phone booth with a mirror without complexion, which would allow your wife to move freely in the streets without teasing innocent men with the beautiful curves of her hundred and five kilos (measured without the phone booth), without having the disadvantages of the niqab which lets glimpse licentious eyes.

---

632. *The Qur'an, op. cit.* sura XXIV, verses 31 and 60, pp. 434 and 439; sura XXXIII, verses 53, 55 and 59, pp. 522-523.

Question 13:

If Muhammad, after having passed from polytheism to monotheism, had lived long enough to change his mind again, and in a final mystical crisis, deny the existence of God, would you still believe in the divine origin of his revelation?

    A - well no, hey, asshole;

    B - Yes, Muhammad is the messenger of God;

    C - uh, well, I don't know, it's a weird question.

Question 14:

If approximately 1% of the population is affected by dissociative disorders, it can be inferred that :

    A - God speaks to 1% of the population;

    B - we should encourage the progress of neuropsychiatry to treat these unfortunate people;

    C - Muhammad would have known what to do to cure them.

Question 15:

When Muhammad made his ablutions, all the submissives rushed to do them, when he spat, all the Muslims spat...[633] If Muhammad had touched his elbow with his tongue, what would you have done?

    A - you would have considered this historical fact as a simple accident, and you show yourself strong enough psychologically not to touch your elbow with your tongue - but eventually the heel;

---

633. HICHÂM (Ibn), *op. cit.* p. 303.

B - you would have touched your elbow with your tongue, even if it is not given to everyone;

C - you would feel free to touch any part of the body at any time. That's how you are. Free in your head.

Question 16:

Let's talk about metaphysics. If Muhammad tells you that everything has a cause, and that this single cause is God, your reaction is the following:

A - you are teasing, even if he gets angry[634], and you ask him: what is the cause of this single cause?

B - you don't understand anything, but you trust the one who looked into it, he probably went to see ;

C - the problem of the cause of the world seems to you to be solved, thank you Muhammad.

Question 17:

Like the Prophet, you have a love at first sight. You have found your soul mate, she is beautiful and submissive, you are going to marry her, she has :

A - six years;

B - already nine years old, but you will be able to consummate the marriage on the spot;

C - at least eighteen years old, which is the age to make an informed decision.

---

634. See HUSSEIN (Mahmoud), *op. cit.* volume II, p. 71.

RECREATION: TEST YOUR SUBMISSION SKILLS

Question 18:

Concerning the expression *"Inch'Allah"*, you think that :

> A - it is a simple cultural expression which marks the attachment to Islam, useless to take it at face value;
>
> B - you can replace it with "If Jean-René wants to", the effect is the same;
>
> C - you must pronounce it before any action in order to have any chance of it being carried out.

Question 19:

On the one hand, Muhammad authorizes consanguineous marriages between first cousins[635], on the other hand, science teaches us that "consanguineous marriages and especially those between first cousins multiply the risks of seeing an anomaly appear"[636]:

> A - when in doubt, if possible, we might as well move away from the family, Muhammad only implicitly authorizes this kind of marriage, without forcing it;
>
> B - you marry your cousin, you have known her since she was a little girl, she was already pretty, she is a good believer, she seems easier to seduce than a stranger, we have always done this in the village, Muhammad would

---

635. See *Le Coran, op. cit.* pp. 96-97.
636. DELAHAYE (Marie-Claude), *Guide pratique de la femme enceinte*, Paris, Marabout, 2000, p. 75.

have done the same and your babies will be normal if God wants it;

C - preferably, you try to meet a woman from another culture and speaking a foreign language, characteristics that offer so many riches to pass on to your future child, not to mention your personal joy in discovering a different civilization.

Question 20:

Muhammad claimed to confirm the previous prophets[637], like Moses who forbade murder and theft[638], or Jesus who encouraged forgiveness of enemies[639]. If the same Muhammad incited you to the holy war by the sword:

A - you would go to the *jihad with* a sword in hand, paradise is promised to the martyrs[640];

B - you would go to *jihad* by word of mouth, without killing anyone, and you would return home after forgiving your enemies;

C - you would not go to *jihad,* and you would open a treatise on logic to check some basic rules.

Results: Calculate the points you've earned, and read on to find out if you'll get your ticket to heaven!

---

637. *The Qur'an, op. cit,* Sura XLVI, "Al 'Ahaqaf", verse 12, p. 623; Sura XLVI, verse 30, p. 627.
638. The Bible, Exodus, chapter XX, verses 13 and 15.
639. See especially The Bible, Matthew, chapter VI, verses 14-15.
640. See in particular HICHAM (Ibn), *op. cit.* pp. 203-204.

	1	2	3	4	5	6	7	8	9	10	11	12	13	14	15	16	17	18	19	20
A	0	2	1	2	2	1	2	0	1	2	2	0	0	1	1	0	2	1	1	2
B	1	1	2	1	1	0	1	2	2	0	1	1	2	0	2	1	1	0	2	1
C	2	0	0	0	0	2	0	1	0	1	0	2	1	2	0	2	0	2	0	0

You have more than thirty points:

You have won. You are submitted. The houris and glasses of water are yours. You love to be told what to do, you don't like to take the initiative and you can die a martyr's death for the cause of God. You just have to hope for an afterlife, an oil field under your land, or that the rich countries will lack manpower.

Conclusion: Pray at the mosque or move to a country run by radical Islamists.

You have between ten and thirty points:

You are in the danger zone. Your heart swings between the mass delirium of child-humanity and the scientific progress of adult-humanity.

You have less than ten points:

Sorry, you lost. You are unsubmissive. You will not go to heaven, especially since it does not exist. You dare to think freely. You are stubbornly trying to contribute to the general progress of humanity through democratic discussion and the slow construction of a better world, but only on earth.

TABLE OF CONTENTS